Selling on eBay

A No-Nonsense Guide to Profitable Selling

Richard Lowe

The Writing King

Selling on eBay: A No-Nonsense Guide to Profitable Selling

Copyright © 2026 by Richard G Lowe

Table of Contents

See books by Richard Lowe at

https://masterofworlds.com

Get free publishing insights and industry updates at

https://thewritingking.substack.com

For ghostwriting and book coaching services see

https://thewritingking.com

Disclaimer

This book is for educational and informational purposes only. The author is not affiliated with eBay Inc. and this book is not endorsed by eBay. eBay policies, fees, and procedures change frequently, and readers should verify current requirements before implementing any strategies discussed in this book.

The information provided reflects the author's personal experience and opinions and should not be considered as professional financial, legal, or business advice. Readers should consult with qualified professionals regarding their specific situations and business decisions.

Results may vary significantly based on individual circumstances, market conditions, and eBay policy changes. The author makes no guarantees regarding income potential or business success. Past performance does not guarantee future results.

All business activities involve risk, including the potential for financial loss. Readers assume full responsibility for their business decisions and outcomes. The author and publisher disclaim any liability for losses or damages resulting from the use of information contained in this book.

Trademark and product names mentioned in this book are the property of their respective owners and are used for identification purposes only.

Preface

I started selling on eBay in 2003 when the platform still felt like a digital garage sale where regular people sold their extra stuff to other regular people who appreciated finding unique items at reasonable prices. Those innocent days disappeared faster than common sense during a Black Friday sale.

This book exists because eBay transformed from a simple auction site into a corporate marketplace that favors professional sellers with deep pockets and sophisticated systems over the individual entrepreneurs who built the platform's original success. The friendly community of buyers and sellers got replaced by an algorithm-driven environment where visibility costs money and policy violations can destroy years of business building overnight.

Most eBay selling guides come from people who either never built substantial businesses on the platform or stopped selling before eBay's corporate evolution made their advice obsolete. They peddle outdated strategies that worked when eBay cared about individual sellers and competition was manageable.

I wrote this book from the perspective of someone who lived through eBay's transformation and adapted business strategies to survive in the platform's increasingly hostile environment. The advice comes from real experience dealing with policy changes, algorithm updates, and enforcement actions that destroyed other sellers who couldn't adapt quickly enough.

This isn't a cheerleading manual promising easy money and effortless success. eBay selling has become a sophisticated business challenge that demands professional approaches, systematic thinking, and realistic expectations about the time and effort required to build sustainable operations.

My goal is helping you understand modern eBay reality while providing practical strategies that work within current constraints instead of fighting against them. Success is still possible, but it requires understanding the game has changed completely from the simple auction site that attracted millions of casual sellers who thought online selling would always be easy.

Introduction

Remember when eBay felt like a digital garage sale where you might stumble across someone's grandmother's china or a rare comic book tucked between dusty baseball cards? Those days are mostly gone, swept away by algorithm updates and corporate efficiency measures that somehow managed to squeeze the magic right out of the experience.

When I published the first edition of this book back in 2015, eBay still had some of that frontier spirit. Sure, it was already a mature marketplace, but sellers could still carve out quirky niches and build genuine relationships with buyers who'd return week after week to see what treasures you'd uncovered. The platform felt more human then, less like a sterile corporate machine designed to extract maximum fees from every transaction.

> ◆ **Personal Experience:** eBay used to be perfect for decluttering your life and making real money doing it. I once made $25,000 in a single year selling over 1,000 items that had been collecting dust in closets, on shelves, and tucked away in corners for decades. But rising fees and declining traffic have made casual selling much less profitable than it used to be.

Fast-forward to 2025, and eBay has transformed into something I barely recognize. The original edition became a Kindle bestseller and helped thousands of people start selling, but honestly, following that old playbook today would be like trying to navigate with a map from the horse-and-buggy era. The rules have changed, the players have changed, and frankly, some of the soul has been corporatized right out of the platform.

The New eBay Reality

PayPal is gone, replaced by eBay's managed payments system that works efficiently but lacks the scrappy independence that made the old setup feel less corporate. Mobile traffic now dominates, with over 60% of buyers shopping on devices smaller than a paperback book, which means your carefully crafted desktop listings might as well be invisible.

Amazon's relentless efficiency has trained buyers to expect miracles. Free shipping, next-day delivery, hassle-free returns - these aren't luxuries anymore but basic expectations that every seller must somehow meet while still turning a profit. Social media platforms have muscled into the selling space, fragmenting attention and making it harder to build the kind of loyal customer base that sustained sellers in eBay's golden years.

The global supply chain hiccups of recent years created opportunities for nimble sellers, but they also revealed just how fragile our interconnected selling world has become. One shipping delay in Shenzhen can torpedo your seller metrics in suburban Ohio.

Yet here's the thing that keeps me cautiously optimistic: eBay remains one of the few platforms where regular people can still build something meaningful. You don't need a computer science degree or venture capital backing. You don't need to crack the code of some social media algorithm that changes weekly. eBay provides the traffic and the infrastructure - you just need to understand how to work within its current reality rather than mourning what it used to be.

Finding Your Place in the Machine

This book covers territory from absolute beginner basics through advanced automation techniques that would have seemed like science fiction a decade ago. I've organized it so newcomers can start at the beginning and work through systematically, while veteran sellers can jump to whatever section addresses their current problems.

★ **Pro Tip:** Even experienced sellers should skim the basics chapters - the fundamentals have shifted more than you might realize.

The dropshipping section reflects a reality that didn't exist when I wrote the first edition. Back then, dropshipping was mostly a sketchy side hustle. Now it's a legitimate business model, though one riddled with pitfalls that can destroy your account faster than you can say "policy violation."

> ▲ **Caution:** The scams and protection sections aren't optional reading - they're survival guides for a marketplace that's become increasingly sophisticated in both its opportunities and its dangers.

What Success Looks Like Now

A profitable eBay business in 2025 requires mastering product research tools that didn't exist ten years ago, optimizing listings for mobile-first buyers, and navigating fee structures that change more often than fashion trends. Customer service expectations have evolved from "thanks for the quick shipping" to demanding Amazon-level perfection from sellers working out of spare bedrooms.

> ■ **Danger Zone:** One negative feedback or policy violation can trigger algorithmic penalties that take months to recover from, if you recover at all.

The strategies in this book come from real sellers operating in today's marketplace, not nostalgic memories of how things used to work. Some techniques I've learned through expensive mistakes that I'd rather you avoid. Others come from the community of sellers who've adapted and thrived despite eBay's transformation into something more corporate and less forgiving than the platform we fell in love with.

The magic isn't completely gone - you just have to work harder to find it. Sometimes you'll still get that email from a buyer thanking you for helping them complete a collection or find something they'd been searching for everywhere. Those moments remind you why this whole crazy business is still worth doing.

Let's figure out how to make it work in the world we live in now, not the one we wish we still had.

PART I: Getting Started

Chapter 1: eBay Fundamentals. What's Changed

Pierre Omidyar probably didn't imagine his little experiment in online person-to-person trading would eventually become a soulless corporate juggernaut obsessed with extracting fees from every conceivable transaction. Back in 1995, eBay felt like a community where real people sold real stuff to other real people who genuinely wanted it. Now it feels more like a casino where the house always wins and sellers are just another revenue stream to optimize.

The bones of eBay remain the same: people post stuff for sale, other people buy it, money changes hands. But everything around those bones has been rebuilt, reengineered, and algorithmically optimized until the original spirit of the place has been sanitized into corporate efficiency. Understanding what's changed isn't just helpful for success, it's essential for survival in a marketplace that's become far less forgiving of mistakes.

The Managed Payments Revolution

The biggest shock for returning sellers is discovering that PayPal has been booted from its throne. For nearly two decades, PayPal was eBay's payment processing partner, and while the relationship was often rocky, it gave sellers some independence from eBay's direct control. You could build relationships with customers through PayPal, maintain some financial autonomy, and frankly, the fees were more predictable.

◆ **Personal Experience:** PayPal is gone, and honestly, good riddance. eBay became much simpler to use once they started handling payments themselves - no more juggling between two different platforms, no more PayPal's quirky dispute process, and no more wondering which company was responsible when something went wrong.

eBay's managed payments system launched in 2018 and became mandatory by 2021, fundamentally changing how money flows through the platform. Instead of buyers paying you through PayPal, eBay now collects all payments and deposits your earnings directly into your bank account. The company touts this as simpler and more streamlined, which it is, but it also means eBay has total control over your money from the moment a buyer clicks "purchase" until funds hit your account.

> ★ **Pro Tip:** Payouts now happen daily instead of waiting for manual transfers, which improves cash flow for active sellers.

The fee structure shifted too. Instead of separate eBay listing fees and PayPal processing fees, everything is bundled into eBay's final value fees. For most categories, you're looking at roughly 10-15% of your total sale price, including shipping. The math often works out similarly to the old system, but the psychological impact of seeing one larger fee instead of two smaller ones hits differently.

Mobile Has Eaten Everything

More than half of eBay's traffic comes from mobile devices, and mobile shoppers behave completely differently from desktop browsers.

Mobile buyers scroll fast, read less, and make quicker decisions. They're often shopping during commercial breaks, waiting in line, or killing time between meetings. Your gorgeous desktop layout becomes a cramped, hard-to-navigate mess on a phone screen. Product photos that looked crisp on a monitor become tiny thumbnails that buyers squint at while riding the subway.

This shift has profound implications for how you create listings. Long, detailed descriptions that worked beautifully in 2015 now feel like walls of text that mobile buyers will skip entirely. The first photo in your listing becomes even more crucial because it might be the only one buyers see before deciding whether to tap for more details.

┌───┐
│ ▲ **Caution:** eBay's mobile app doesn't display all the custom HTML formatting that desktop users see, so those fancy templates you paid for might be worthless. │
└───┘

The Algorithm's Invisible Hand

eBay's search algorithm has become a black box that makes Google's PageRank look transparent. The platform now uses machine learning to determine which listings to show buyers, and the factors it considers have multiplied exponentially. Your listing's visibility depends not just on keywords and price, but on your seller performance metrics, shipping speed, return policy, customer service ratings, and dozens of other variables that eBay tracks but doesn't fully disclose.

This algorithmic approach means that two identical items posted by different sellers can have wildly different visibility in search results. A new seller with no feedback history might find their listings buried on page 10, while an established seller with strong metrics gets prime real estate on page 1. The rich get richer, and newcomers face an uphill battle that didn't exist when search results were primarily determined by auction end times and keyword relevance.

The algorithm also responds to buyer behavior in real-time. If people click on your listing but don't buy, that signals poor conversion and can hurt your future visibility. If buyers purchase from you but then return items frequently, the algorithm interprets that as customer dissatisfaction and reduces your reach. Every interaction becomes a data point that feeds back into your long-term success or failure on the platform.

The Amazon Effect

Amazon's dominance in e-commerce has fundamentally reset buyer expectations across all online marketplaces. Customers now expect free shipping, hassle-free returns, and lightning-fast delivery times, regardless of whether they're buying from a billion-dollar corporation or someone selling out of their garage. This creates an impossible standard for small sellers who can't absorb shipping costs or maintain warehouse networks.

The "Prime effect" is particularly brutal. Amazon Prime has trained millions of customers to expect free two-day shipping as a basic service rather than a premium offering. When these customers shop on eBay, they often abandon carts when they see shipping charges that reflect the actual cost of getting packages from point A to point B. Sellers find themselves forced to build shipping costs into item prices and offer "free shipping" to remain competitive, which distorts pricing and makes it harder to offer competitive deals on heavy or bulky items.

> ■ **Danger Zone:** Trying to compete directly with Amazon on shipping speed and cost is a losing game that will bankrupt small sellers.

Social Commerce Fragmentation

The rise of social media marketplaces has scattered potential customers across dozens of platforms. Facebook Marketplace, Instagram Shopping, TikTok Shop, Poshmark, Mercari, and countless other apps now compete for the same buyers who once defaulted to eBay for their online shopping needs. Each platform has its own culture, fee structure, and best practices, forcing sellers to choose between spreading themselves thin across multiple channels or focusing deeply on one platform and potentially missing opportunities elsewhere.

This fragmentation is particularly painful for sellers of collectibles, vintage items, and niche products where eBay historically dominated. A collector looking for vintage Star Wars figures might check eBay, but they're just as likely to browse Facebook groups, Instagram hashtags, or specialized forums. The concentrated audience that made eBay powerful in its early days has been dispersed across the broader internet.

Supply Chain Realities

Global supply chain disruptions over the past few years exposed how interconnected and fragile the modern selling world has become. Sellers who built businesses around importing products from overseas discovered that a factory closure in Vietnam or a shipping backup in Los Angeles could destroy months of planning. The "just in time" inventory management that worked beautifully in stable times became a liability when nothing arrived on time.

These disruptions also created opportunities for sellers nimble enough to adapt. Local sourcing became more attractive when international shipping became unreliable. Sellers who maintained diverse supplier relationships weathered storms better than those dependent on single sources. The sellers who thrived were those who built flexibility into their operations instead of optimizing for efficiency at the expense of resilience.

What Still Works

Despite all these changes, some fundamentals remain constant. Good customer service still matters. Quality photos still sell products. Accurate descriptions still prevent problems. Competitive pricing still drives sales. The core skills of selling haven't disappeared, they've just become table stakes in a more competitive environment.

eBay still offers advantages that newer platforms can't match. The buyer base is massive and established. The search traffic is organic, you don't need to build an audience from scratch. The feedback system, while imperfect, provides social proof that helps buyers trust unknown sellers. The platform handles payment processing, fraud protection, and dispute resolution, removing administrative headaches that plague sellers on less mature platforms.

The key is understanding that success on modern eBay requires playing by today's rules, not yesterday's. The sellers who thrive are those who've adapted their strategies to work with algorithms instead of against them, who've optimized for mobile shoppers instead of clinging to desktop-era practices, and who've found ways to meet elevated customer expectations without destroying their profit margins.

The magic isn't completely gone. You just have to work harder to find it, and you need to understand the new landscape well enough to navigate it successfully. eBay in 2025 is more corporate and less forgiving than it was — but it's still one of the best places for regular people to build profitable online businesses. You just need to know how the game is played now.

Creating an eBay seller account used to take five minutes. Now eBay treats every new seller as a potential fraud risk until the verification process decides otherwise — and that process has grown considerably more involved than picking a username and confirming an email address.

The onboarding process now involves identity verification, financial background checks, and a probationary period where your account operates under selling limits that can torpedo early momentum if you don't understand them. Plan for this rather than being surprised by it.

The Verification Gauntlet

It starts innocently enough with basic account creation, but eBay's verification requirements now resemble something from a government security clearance application. You'll need to provide your Social Security number, driver's license information, bank account details, and sometimes even additional documentation proving you are who you claim to be. The platform uses third-party verification services that cross-reference your information against databases you didn't know existed.

The process can take anywhere from a few minutes to several weeks, depending on how cleanly your information matches what's in various corporate and government databases. If you've moved recently, changed your name, or have any discrepancies in your credit history, expect delays that feel like bureaucratic purgatory. Some sellers get stuck in verification limbo for months, watching potential selling opportunities slip away while they wait for some algorithm to decide they're legitimate.

> ■ **Danger Zone:** Never attempt to create multiple seller accounts or use false information during verification. eBay's fraud detection systems will flag you permanently, and appealing these decisions is nearly impossible.

Choosing Your Seller Identity

Your username becomes your brand on eBay, and unlike the early days when you could change it on a whim, you're stuck with whatever you choose. The platform discourages username changes because they confuse buyers and break the feedback continuity that makes the reputation system work. Pick something professional that won't embarrass you when you're doing $50,000 in annual sales.

Avoid usernames that scream "amateur" or contain references to temporary situations. "CollegeKid2025" might seem clever now, but it'll feel dated in six months. Names with excessive numbers, underscores, or random characters look spammy to buyers who've been trained to associate legitimate sellers with clean, professional usernames. Think about how your username will look in buyer messages, on invoices, and in search results.

> ★ **Pro Tip:** If your ideal username is taken, try adding your city, state, or specialty instead of random numbers. "VintageToysTexas" looks more professional than "VintageToys147."

The Banking Connection

Managed payments requires linking a bank account that can receive daily deposits, and eBay is surprisingly picky about which banks they'll accept. Most major banks work fine, but some smaller credit unions or online-only banks get rejected for reasons eBay doesn't clearly explain. You'll also need to verify your bank account through micro-deposits, a process that can take several business days.

> ◆ **Personal Experience:** Micro deposits aren't the hassle they sound like. eBay just sends two tiny transactions (usually under 10 cents each) to your bank account. Once they show up, you log into eBay and enter those exact amounts to prove the account is really yours. Takes maybe five minutes once the deposits clear.

The bank account you link becomes permanently associated with your seller identity, and changing it later requires going through additional verification steps. If you're planning to open a dedicated business account for your eBay sales, do it before starting the seller registration process. Trying to switch banks mid-stream can trigger security reviews that freeze your account for weeks.

Understanding Selling Limits

New sellers face monthly selling limits that start embarrassingly low, often just $500 in total sales or 10 items, whichever comes first. These limits exist to prevent fraud and minimize eBay's exposure to problem sellers, but they also make it nearly impossible to build meaningful momentum in your first few months. The limits increase automatically based on your performance, but the pace feels glacial when you're eager to grow.

> ▲ **Caution:** Hitting your selling limits doesn't just prevent new listings, it can also prevent you from accepting offers on existing items or relisting unsold inventory.

You can request limit increases, but eBay's approval process considers factors you can't control: your credit history, the length of time your account has existed, and mysterious "risk assessment" calculations. Some sellers see their limits increase steadily month by month, while others get stuck at the same low limits for six months or more despite perfect performance metrics.

> ◆ **Personal Experience:** My selling limits started ridiculously low at just a few thousand dollars. This year, eBay raised my limit to over $1 million, which feels almost insulting - like they're taunting me with limits I'll never use. I'd love to sell something worth a million bucks, but I don't exactly have any Picassos lying around.

Payment Schedule Realities

Managed payments deposits your earnings daily, which sounds great until you discover that eBay holds funds from new sellers for longer periods to reduce their risk exposure. Your first few sales might have funds held for 21 days after delivery confirmation, regardless of how quickly the buyer receives their item or how positive their feedback is.

The hold periods gradually decrease as you build selling history and positive feedback, but the transition happens slowly and inconsistently. Some sellers find their funds released immediately after their first month, while others deal with extended holds for several months. eBay's communication about why funds are held and when they'll be released is frustratingly vague, often citing "standard business practices" without explaining the actual criteria being used.

These payment delays can create serious cash flow problems for sellers who need to reinvest earnings into new inventory. Planning your business around immediate access to sales proceeds is a recipe for frustration and potential failure during the critical early months when you're establishing your seller reputation.

Store Subscription Decisions

eBay pushes new sellers toward paid store subscriptions almost immediately, promising lower fees and better visibility for a monthly fee. The basic store subscription costs $7.95 per month and does provide some genuine benefits: more free listings, slightly lower final value fees, and access to additional marketing tools. But for truly new sellers still operating under severe selling limits, the monthly fee might exceed the savings for months.

> ◆ **Personal Experience:** I declutter about once a year and always renew my store subscription for those few months when I'm rummaging through everything I own. The subscription easily pays for itself during these selling sprees, plus it opens up better promotional tools that help move inventory faster when you're trying to clear out years of accumulated stuff.

The store subscription decision depends heavily on your expected selling volume and average item price. If you're planning to sell high-value items occasionally, the monthly store fee might never pay for itself. If you're planning to move lots of lower-priced inventory, the fee savings kick in much sooner. The challenge is making this decision before you know what your actual selling patterns will look like.

Tax Information Setup

eBay now handles tax collection and remittance in most states, which simplifies compliance but adds complexity to the initial account setup. You'll need to provide tax identification information, choose how you want sales tax handled, and understand how the managed payments system affects your tax reporting responsibilities.

The platform automatically collects sales tax from buyers in states where you have nexus, which initially meant states where you physically reside or have inventory. But the rules keep expanding, and eBay's interpretation of tax nexus is conservative, meaning they might collect tax in more states than legally required. This protects them from liability but can make your items slightly more expensive to buyers in those states.

Your tax obligations matter because eBay reports your sales to the IRS once you exceed certain thresholds. The reporting requirements changed dramatically in recent years, and many casual sellers discover they owe taxes on income they didn't realize was reportable. Setting up proper record-keeping systems from day one prevents nightmares during tax season.

Privacy And Security Settings

eBay's default privacy settings lean toward transparency, sharing more information about sellers than many people expect. Your feedback profile shows your general location, and buyers can see patterns in your selling history that might reveal more than you intended. Reviewing and adjusting these settings early prevents privacy surprises later.

Two-factor authentication is now strongly recommended and becomes mandatory for sellers who reach certain volume thresholds. Setting it up early prevents disruptions to your selling when eBay eventually forces the requirement. The authentication system works through text messages or authenticator apps, and losing access to your chosen method can lock you out of your account for days.

> ◆ **Personal Experience:** Getting your eBay account hacked is a nightmare that can cost you money and take weeks to resolve. Turn on two-factor authentication, use a strong password, and never let anyone else access your account - even family members. These basic security steps can save you from the headache of dealing with unauthorized listings, hijacked funds, and eBay's painfully slow account recovery process.

Setting up your seller account properly the first time prevents countless headaches later. The process has become more complex and bureaucratic than it used to be, but understanding the requirements and restrictions helps you navigate the system more effectively. Take the time to get everything configured correctly before you start listing items, because changing these fundamental settings later can trigger reviews and restrictions that disrupt your selling momentum.

The magic of eBay used to include how easy it was to get started. That simplicity is gone, replaced by corporate risk management and regulatory compliance requirements. But underneath all the bureaucracy, the fundamental opportunity remains: a massive marketplace where regular people can still build profitable businesses by connecting buyers with products they want.

Chapter 3: Understanding eBay's Fee Structure

eBay fees used to be simple enough to calculate on a napkin. Listing fee, final value fee, done. The current structure has been layered, tiered, categorized, and promotional-discounted into something that requires a spreadsheet to understand and a strong stomach to look at directly. This complexity is not an accident.

The Managed Payments Fee Consolidation

The biggest change since 2015 is the consolidation of eBay and PayPal fees into a single managed payments structure. Instead of paying eBay for listing fees and PayPal for payment processing, everything gets bundled into eBay's final value fees. This sounds simpler until you realize that eBay now controls the entire fee calculation and can adjust rates without external pressure from PayPal's pricing.

Final value fees now range from 3.49% to 15% of your total sale price, including shipping costs. The percentage depends on your category, item price, store subscription level, and whether you meet various performance thresholds that eBay doesn't clearly publicize. A vintage guitar might incur different fees than a new guitar, and the same guitar sold by a Top Rated Seller gets charged differently than one sold by a new seller with no feedback history.

◆ **Personal Experience:** I once sold a $10,000 book set consisting of 50 volumes that required five boxes to ship. eBay called me every single day to make sure I shipped it and that it arrived safely - they were clearly nervous about such a high-value transaction. The good news was that eBay's fee cap kicked in, so instead of paying $1,000+ in fees, I hit the maximum fee limit for my store subscription level. Those caps are one of the few seller-friendly policies eBay still maintains.

The inclusion of shipping costs in fee calculations fundamentally changed pricing strategies. When eBay charged fees only on item prices, sellers could minimize fees by charging low item prices with high shipping costs. Now that shipping charges are included in fee calculations, this strategy backfires by increasing your total fees while making your items less competitive in search results that favor "free shipping."

> ★ **Pro Tip:** Use eBay's fee calculator religiously before listing items. The actual fees can vary significantly from the advertised rates depending on your specific situation.

Category-Specific Fee Variations

eBay's fee structure varies dramatically across different categories, supposedly reflecting the platform's costs and competitive dynamics in each market segment. Electronics and technology items often face higher fees because of increased fraud risks and return rates, while collectibles and antiques might enjoy lower fees because those markets traditionally belonged to eBay's core strengths.

The category system itself has become a strategic consideration for sellers. The same item might legitimately fit into multiple categories with different fee structures, and choosing the right category can significantly impact your profitability. A vintage band t-shirt could go in Clothing, Collectibles, or Entertainment Memorabilia, each with different fee rates and different buyer audiences.

Some categories have special fee structures that can dramatically impact profitability. Automotive parts, for example, have different fee caps than general merchandise. Real estate has its own fee schedule. Business and industrial items often have different rates than consumer goods. These variations can mean the difference between profitable sales and working for free.

> ▲ **Caution:** eBay actively monitors for sellers who consistently list items in wrong categories to avoid higher fees. This can result in policy violations that hurt your account standing.

Store Subscription Fee Benefits

eBay's store subscriptions promise fee reductions that can justify the monthly costs, but the math only works if you understand exactly how the discounts apply. The basic store at $7.95 per month provides modest fee reductions that might save you money if you sell more than a few hundred dollars monthly. The premium and anchor store levels offer more substantial savings but require much higher sales volumes to break even.

Store subscription benefits extend beyond fee discounts to include more free listings, advanced marketing tools, and better search placement. But these additional benefits are hard to quantify, making it difficult to determine whether the store subscription actually improves your bottom line. Some sellers swear by their store subscriptions while others consider them an expensive placebo that doesn't meaningfully impact sales.

The store subscription decision becomes more complex when you consider that eBay occasionally offers promotional rates or temporary upgrades. Timing your subscription around these promotions can provide better value, but the promotional terms often include restrictions that limit their usefulness for serious sellers.

Insertion Fee Complexities

While final value fees get most of the attention, insertion fees for listing items can add up quickly for sellers with large inventories or low-priced items. eBay provides a certain number of free listings monthly based on your account status and store subscription level, but exceeding those limits triggers insertion fees that range from 30 cents to several dollars per listing.

The free listing allocations reset monthly and don't roll over, creating a use-it-or-lose-it dynamic that encourages constant listing activity. Sellers often find themselves rushing to use up their free listings at month-end, leading to poor listing quality or inappropriate timing for certain items.

Auction-style listings generally receive more free listing allowances than fixed-price listings, reflecting eBay's preference for the auction format that built their early success. But auction listings require more active management and carry higher risks of items selling below desired prices, making the fee savings potentially meaningless if you're accepting low final sale prices.

Optional Feature Fees

eBay offers numerous optional listing features that promise better visibility and higher sale prices, but most of these features cost extra and provide questionable returns on investment. Bold listings, subtitle additions, gallery plus features, and listing upgrades can easily add $5-10 to your listing costs before you sell anything.

Promoted listings represent the newest and most significant optional fee category. These paid advertisements promise better search placement in exchange for additional fees calculated as percentages of final sale prices. The promoted listings system operates like an auction where sellers bid against each other for visibility, driving up costs while providing uncertain benefits.

The psychology of optional features creates a trap for sellers who feel pressured to purchase every available upgrade to improve their chances of success. eBay's interface presents these options as recommendations, making them feel necessary when they're often just additional revenue streams for the platform.

> ■ **Danger Zone:** Optional listing features rarely provide returns that justify their costs. Start with basic listings and only add paid features after you have data proving they improve your results.

International Transaction Fees

Selling internationally introduces additional fee layers that can quickly erode profitability on cross-border transactions. Currency conversion fees, international payment processing charges, and Global Shipping Program costs combine to create fee structures that often exceed 20% of sale prices for international transactions.

The Global Shipping Program, which eBay promotes as simplifying international sales, adds its own fee layer while removing seller control over the international shipping experience. Buyers pay higher shipping costs, sellers receive lower net proceeds, and eBay captures additional fees for supporting the transaction.

> ◆ **Personal Experience:** I absolutely love eBay's Global Shipping Program. It couldn't be simpler - you box up your item normally, slap on the eBay shipping label, and send it to their US hub. From there, they handle all the international shipping, customs paperwork, and regulatory headaches. You get paid immediately without worrying about international delivery delays or customs issues that used to make overseas selling a nightmare.

Currency conversion rates used by eBay's managed payments system often include spreads that favor the platform over sellers. The conversion happens automatically when international buyers purchase your items, and the rates used might be less favorable than what you could obtain through other currency exchange services.

Volume Incentive Programs

eBay offers fee discounts for high-volume sellers through programs like Top Rated Seller status and various seller levels that provide percentage discounts on final value fees. These programs sound attractive but require meeting performance standards for shipping time, customer service metrics, and return policies that might not be feasible for smaller sellers.

The Top Rated Seller program offers final value fee discounts up to 10% in some categories, but qualifying requires maintaining metrics that can be difficult to sustain. Above-standard delivery speed, accepting returns, and maintaining high customer satisfaction scores all factor into program eligibility, and losing status can happen quickly if your metrics slip.

Volume thresholds for fee discounts keep increasing as eBay raises the bar for qualification. Discount percentages that were available to sellers doing $10,000 monthly a few years ago now require much higher volumes, reflecting the platform's focus on attracting larger, more professional sellers at the expense of smaller operations.

Fee Calculation Examples

The best way to see how fees compound is to work through real examples that show how various charges interact. A $100 item sold with $10 shipping through a basic store subscription might incur fees that total $14-16 when you include final value fees, payment processing, and any optional features you selected.

The same $100 item sold by a Top Rated Seller with an anchor store subscription might incur total fees of $10-12, a meaningful difference that compounds across hundreds of transactions. But achieving Top Rated status and justifying an anchor store subscription requires sales volumes and performance metrics that might take years to develop.

Fee calculations become more complex when promotions and special offers get involved. eBay frequently runs listing promotions that provide additional free listings or reduced final value fees, but these promotions often come with restrictions that limit their usefulness or create timing pressures that force suboptimal selling decisions.

The Hidden Cost of Returns

eBay's managed returns policy creates fee implications that many sellers don't understand until they experience them firsthand. When buyers return items, eBay refunds their payment but doesn't refund your final value fees unless the return is due to your error or item misrepresentation. This means returns for buyer's remorse or sizing issues cost you the fees on transactions that ultimately generated no revenue.

Return shipping costs add another layer of expense that can completely eliminate profit margins on lower-priced items. Even when buyers pay return shipping costs, the time and effort required to process returns, inspect returned items, and relist inventory creates hidden costs that fee calculations don't capture.

> ◆ **Personal Experience:** Returns are expensive and time-consuming. For anything under $25, I usually just write it off and let the buyer keep the item rather than deal with return shipping costs and hassle. The math rarely works out in your favor on low-value items. But if a buyer is being a jerk or clearly trying to scam me, I'll make them go through the full return process on principle.

The return rate varies dramatically across categories and price points, making it difficult to budget for these costs. Electronics and clothing typically have higher return rates than collectibles or handmade items, but individual sellers can experience return patterns that don't match category averages.

Budgeting For Fee Reality

Sustainable eBay selling means budgeting for total transaction costs that often reach 15-20% of sale prices when you include all fees, return costs, and optional features. New sellers who budget based only on advertised final value fees often discover their profit margins disappearing once they account for the full cost structure.

Fee planning gets complicated when your inventory spans different price ranges. A $200 item and an $8 item have completely different fee profiles — percentage fees favor higher prices, minimum fees punish low-price sales. Run the numbers separately for each type of item you sell rather than assuming one margin percentage applies across the board.

eBay's rates also move. Fee structures that made certain products profitable can shift without warning, and the promotional rates they offer come and go. Don't lock yourself into pricing based on a fee structure that might not exist in six months.

The napkin math that worked on the old eBay doesn't work anymore. The platform is more expensive, more complex, and less transparent about exactly what you'll pay. Know your real numbers, build them into your pricing from the start, and revisit them whenever eBay announces a change.

Chapter 4: Basic Listing Creation

One of my most memorable local sales involved a collector who contacted me about purchasing my entire collection of plastic model kits. I had accumulated over a hundred models during my younger years, ranging from Star Wars ships to military aircraft, all sitting in boxes gathering dust in a closet.

The buyer arrived with cash and spent two hours examining every kit, checking for missing pieces and evaluating condition. We negotiated item by item, with him offering varying prices based on rarity and completeness. Some common models went for $5-10, while a few rare Star Wars kits commanded $40-50 each.

The entire transaction netted me around $800 for items I'd forgotten I owned. More importantly, it taught me that local pickup sales can work well for bulk collections when shipping costs would make individual sales unprofitable. The buyer saved money by avoiding shipping, and I avoided the time and expense of photographing and listing each model separately.

This experience showed me that sometimes the best deals come from selling collections as lots rather than individual items, especially when dealing with knowledgeable collectors who understand value and are willing to pay fairly for convenience.

Modern eBay listings aren't just product descriptions, they're digital marketing campaigns that need to perform across multiple devices, satisfy algorithmic ranking factors, and convert browsers into buyers in an attention economy where you have maybe three seconds to make an impression. The platform's listing tools have evolved to support this complexity, but they've also created new ways to fail that didn't exist when eBay was simpler and more forgiving.

The Title Optimization Game

Your listing title carries more weight than any other single element — it drives search visibility and buyer clicks simultaneously. eBay's algorithm uses title keywords as primary ranking factors, while buyers scan titles to decide whether your item deserves their attention. This dual audience creates constant tension between writing for machines and writing for humans.

The 80-character title limit forces brutal prioritization of the most important keywords while maintaining readability. Every character matters when you're trying to include brand name, model number, size, color, condition, and compelling descriptors that make buyers want to click. The math rarely works out cleanly, leaving you with impossible choices about what information to sacrifice.

Keyword stuffing used to work when eBay's algorithm was simpler, but modern search systems penalize titles that read like random word salads. "Nike Air Jordan Retro Basketball Shoes Sneakers Men Size 10 Red Black White New" might capture searches but feels robotic compared to "Nike Air Jordan 1 Retro High OG Chicago Size 10 - Brand New in Box." The challenge is finding the sweet spot between keyword density and natural language that real people want to read.

> ★ **Pro Tip:** Research completed listings in your category to see which title formats perform best, then adapt the successful patterns to your specific items.

Photo Requirements For Mobile Success

Photography has transformed from nice-to-have into make-or-break for listing success. Mobile shoppers scroll through search results looking at thumbnail images, often making decisions based purely on photos without reading titles or descriptions. Your first photo needs to work as a tiny thumbnail, a medium-sized search result, and a full-screen mobile image.

The technical requirements have gotten more demanding as screen resolutions improved and buyer expectations increased. Photos need to be bright enough to look good on phones in direct sunlight, detailed enough to zoom cleanly on high-resolution displays, and composed to work across aspect ratios from square thumbnails to wide desktop monitors.

eBay's photo hosting handles the technical scaling, but you're responsible for providing source images that look professional across all these contexts. The days of acceptable blurry photos taken with potato-quality cameras are long gone, replaced by buyer expectations trained by Amazon's professional product photography and Instagram's visual culture.

Lighting makes the difference between photos that sell and photos that scroll past unnoticed. Natural daylight near a window beats any artificial lighting setup for color accuracy and overall appeal. The harsh shadows and yellow color casts from indoor lighting make even great products look cheap and unprofessional.

Background choices affect perceived value more than most sellers realize. Clean, neutral backgrounds make items look professional and help them stand out in search results filled with cluttered, distracting photos. White backgrounds work well for most items, but sometimes a lifestyle context helps buyers envision using the product.

> ▲ **Caution:** eBay's mobile app automatically crops photos to fit different screen layouts, so important details positioned at photo edges might get cut off.

Category Selection Strategy

Choosing the right category affects everything from search visibility to fee calculations, but eBay's category structure often feels like it was designed by committees that never talked to each other. The same item might legitimately fit into multiple categories with different audiences, fee structures, and competition levels.

Category browsing has mostly given way to search, but your category choice still affects which related items eBay shows buyers near yours, which listing tools are available, and which search filters apply. A vintage band t-shirt in the wrong category misses the buyers who would have paid the most for it.

The category structure keeps evolving as eBay adds new sections and reorganizes existing ones to match changing shopping patterns. Categories that made sense five years ago might now be buried under new organizational schemes that make them harder for buyers to find through browsing.

Misclassifying items can trigger policy violations that hurt your seller standing, but the boundaries between categories aren't always clear. A vintage band t-shirt could reasonably go in Clothing, Collectibles, or Entertainment Memorabilia depending on how you frame its appeal to buyers.

Condition Descriptions That Matter

eBay's standardized condition options (New, Used, Refurbished, etc.) provide consistency for buyers but don't capture the nuances that affect value and buyer satisfaction. The difference between "very good" and "excellent" condition can be $50 on a collectible item, but eBay's broad categories don't help buyers understand what they're actually getting.

Detailed condition descriptions in your listing text become crucial for setting accurate expectations and preventing returns. Buyers have become more demanding about condition disclosure, partly because return policies have made it easier to send back items that don't match expectations.

Photography can't capture everything that affects condition and value. Scents, functionality issues, wear patterns, and subtle damage often require written descriptions that help buyers make informed decisions. The goal is complete honesty that prevents surprises and disputes.

Condition disclosure affects your legal protection in disputes and return cases. eBay's policies favor buyers in most situations, but accurate condition descriptions provide some protection when buyers try to return items for reasons not disclosed in your listing.

Pricing Psychology for Immediate Sales

Pricing on eBay is not just cost-plus math. Buyer psychology matters, algorithm factors matter, and the difference between $19.99 and $20.00 is more than a penny — it's a different search filter threshold and a different psychological category for the buyer scanning results on their phone.

Always check completed sales, not just active listings. What sellers ask and what buyers pay are completely different numbers in most categories. The active listings show you the competition. The sold listings show you the reality.

Best Offer functionality changes pricing dynamics by allowing negotiation without the complexity of auction formats. Enabling Best Offer can increase engagement and final sale prices, but it also attracts lowball offers that waste time without leading to sales.

◆ **Personal Experience:** I once sold a $200 item in an auction starting at 97 cents after seeing other sellers make a killing with this strategy. Big mistake. The auction ended with a single bid of about $1.50, and I had to sell something valuable for basically nothing. That taught me never to start auctions below my absolute minimum acceptable price, no matter how confident I am about generating bidding wars.

Auction versus Buy It Now pricing strategies depend on item rarity, demand predictability, and your timeline for selling. Auctions can generate excitement and competitive bidding for unique items, but they can also result in disappointingly low final prices when bidding interest doesn't materialize.

■ **Danger Zone:** Starting auctions at extremely low prices to attract attention can backfire spectacularly if bidding competition doesn't develop.

Description Writing for Conversion

Your item description needs to work for buyers reading on phones, tablets, and desktop computers while providing enough detail to prevent returns and disputes. Mobile-first design means front-loading the most important information and using formatting that remains readable on small screens.

Write descriptions for buyers, not for search bots. Include your relevant keywords naturally, but don't stuff them. A description that reads like a keyword list signals to buyers, correctly, that no human being wrote it.

Bullet points and short paragraphs work better than walls of text for mobile readability, but eBay's text formatting tools are limited compared to modern website builders. Simple formatting with clear hierarchy helps buyers find the information they need quickly.

> ◆ **Personal Experience:** My honest descriptions have saved my butt more than once. I sold an item with obvious flaws that I clearly described and photographed. When the buyer complained and opened a case with eBay, I was able to win the dispute because my listing had documented every defect upfront. Being brutally honest in your descriptions isn't just good customer service - it's legal protection when buyers try to pull fast ones.

Honest flaw disclosure protects you from return disputes while building buyer confidence in your credibility. Hiding obvious problems guarantees negative feedback and return hassles, while proactive disclosure often results in sales to buyers who don't mind minor issues.

Shipping Configuration Complexity

Shipping setup has become one of the most complex aspects of listing creation, with calculated shipping, flat rates, free shipping, and local pickup options each creating different buyer experiences and fee implications. The shipping configuration you choose affects search ranking, buyer psychology, and your profit margins.

Free shipping has effectively become the price of entry for competitive search placement. The shipping cost doesn't disappear — you fold it into the item price. The math usually works out the same for the buyer; the psychology works out differently, and eBay's algorithm rewards the free-shipping listing.

Calculated shipping provides accuracy but can scare away buyers when costs seem high compared to free shipping competitors. Package dimensions and weights need to be accurate to prevent billing disputes and customer service issues.

Fast handling time improves search ranking and buyer satisfaction, but committing to same-day or next-day handling creates operational pressure that might not be sustainable for part-time sellers or complex items that require careful packaging.

◆ **Personal Experience:** I once sold 300 bottles of Testors model paint without realizing it qualified as hazardous material. The post office explained I needed special hazmat labeling for anything flammable or chemical-based. It's not complicated once you know the rules, but getting caught shipping hazmat without proper declaration can result in fines.

Return Policy Decisions

eBay's managed return system gives buyers significant power to return items regardless of your stated policy, making return configuration more about managing expectations than controlling actual return outcomes. But your stated policy still influences buyer confidence and search algorithm ranking.

Accepting returns can improve search visibility and buyer confidence enough to increase sales that offset return costs. Buyers often feel more comfortable purchasing from sellers who accept returns, even when they don't intend to use the return option.

Return shipping responsibility affects both buyer perception and your actual costs when returns happen. Offering free return shipping can improve conversion rates but creates direct costs that need to be factored into pricing decisions.

◆ **Personal Experience:** In a decade of selling on eBay, I've had surprisingly few returns, and most were for legitimate reasons like sizing issues or damage during shipping. The handful of sketchy returns were buyers fishing for free merchandise, assuming I wouldn't bother asking for the item back. These scammers are rare, but you need to stay alert and always require actual returns rather than just issuing refunds.

Restocking fees for returned items can help offset processing costs but might discourage sales from buyers who want risk-free purchasing options. The fees also need to be clearly disclosed to be enforceable.

Mobile Preview Testing

Testing how your listings appear on mobile devices before publishing prevents formatting disasters that kill conversion rates. eBay's desktop listing creation tools don't always accurately preview mobile formatting, leading to listings that look great on computers but terrible on phones.

Photo cropping, text formatting, and feature availability all change between desktop and mobile versions of eBay. Important information positioned poorly can become unreadable or invisible on mobile devices where most buyers now shop.

Create on desktop, check on mobile before publishing. What looks organized on a monitor can become a wall of text on a phone screen. This is a ten-second step that prevents listing failures you won't notice until a buyer doesn't click.

Good listings used to mean writing a clear description and taking a decent photo. That's still the foundation. What's been added on top — keyword optimization, mobile layout, algorithm factors — isn't as mysterious as it sounds once you've built a few listings and watched what sells and what doesn't. The fundamentals still drive the results. The rest is tuning.

When I first started selling, I listed a large framed print with glass in an auction. The final bid was $60, and I confidently charged about $10 for shipping without thinking much about the logistics involved.

Shipping a 24x36 framed, glass-covered print turned out to be incredibly difficult. By the time I purchased the special box, adequate padding, tape, postage, and everything else needed, I wound up losing $10 on the deal. Not only did I lose money, but it took a couple of hours to get the thing ready to ship safely.

These days, when I need to ship artwork in frames with glass, I pay for the packing service at the local UPS store. The cost is worth it for the time savings and professional packing that prevents damage during shipping.

Shipping used to mean walking to the post office with a package and hoping it arrived safely. Payment meant waiting for a check to clear. Neither of those is the job anymore. Shipping speed now affects search ranking. Payment processing is automated but eBay controls the timing. Buyers expect Amazon-level service from someone working out of a spare bedroom.

eBay's managed payments system controls money flow while their shipping requirements influence everything from listing visibility to customer satisfaction scores. Understanding these interconnected systems makes the difference between sustainable profits and working for free while subsidizing buyer expectations that have spiraled beyond reason.

Managed Payments Money Flow

eBay collects all payments from buyers and deposits your earnings directly into your bank account, eliminating the PayPal middleman but giving eBay total control over your money. The platform processes credit cards, debit cards, PayPal, Apple Pay,

Google Pay, and other payment methods while you see only the net deposits minus their fees.

This centralized system simplifies some aspects of selling while creating new dependencies that can freeze your business if problems arise. eBay holds the power to delay payouts, freeze accounts, or withhold funds for policy violations, creating cash flow vulnerabilities that didn't exist when PayPal provided some independence from eBay's direct control.

Daily payouts sound appealing until you discover that eBay holds funds from new sellers for extended periods regardless of transaction completion. Your first sales might trigger 21-day fund holds that ignore delivery confirmation, positive feedback, or buyer satisfaction. The platform releases these holds gradually based on account age and performance metrics that remain largely opaque.

Fund holds create serious cash flow challenges for sellers who need to reinvest earnings into new inventory. You might complete successful sales but wait weeks to access the proceeds, making it difficult to maintain inventory levels or respond to market opportunities that require quick capital deployment.

> ★ **Pro Tip:** Set up your business banking before you start selling to make sure smooth payout processing and avoid personal account complications.

Shipping Speed Pressure

Same-day and next-day handling times have become competitive requirements rather than premium services, thanks to Amazon Prime conditioning buyers to expect unrealistic speed from all online sellers. eBay's algorithm rewards fast handling times with better search placement, creating pressure to commit to shipping schedules that might not be sustainable.

Handling time commitments become binding obligations that affect your seller performance metrics and search visibility. Promise next-day handling and fail to ship on time, and eBay's system penalizes your future listings even if the delay resulted from circumstances beyond your control.

Weekend and holiday shipping expectations have expanded as shipping carriers offer seven-day delivery in many markets. Buyers increasingly expect packages to ship on Saturdays and Sundays, creating operational pressure for sellers who want to maintain personal time boundaries while meeting algorithmic performance requirements.

The logistics become more complex when you sell items that require careful packaging, quality inspection, or coordination with suppliers. Committing to same-day handling works fine for simple items stored in your home office but becomes impossible for complex products that need proper preparation time.

Calculated Vs. Flat Rate Shipping

Calculated shipping provides accuracy by using actual package dimensions and destinations to determine real shipping costs, but the complexity can scare away buyers who prefer predictable shipping charges. The system requires accurate weight and dimension measurements that many sellers estimate incorrectly, leading to billing disputes and customer service headaches.

Package size restrictions from shipping carriers create hidden complexities that calculated shipping exposes. A lightweight item might incur high shipping costs because of dimensional weight pricing that charges based on package size rather than actual weight. These unexpected costs can make your items uncompetitive or force you to absorb shipping charges that eliminate profit margins.

Flat rate shipping simplifies buyer decision-making but requires averaging shipping costs across all potential destinations, often resulting in overcharging nearby buyers to subsidize distant shipments. The averaging works when you sell items with predictable sizes and weights but becomes problematic for varied inventory with widely different shipping requirements.

Zone skipping and regional shipping variations make flat rate calculations nearly impossible for sellers with national reach. Shipping a package from California to Nevada costs dramatically less than shipping the same package to Maine, but flat rate pricing forces you to choose between losing money on distant sales or overcharging local buyers.

> ▲ **Caution:** Underestimating shipping costs to appear competitive will destroy your profit margins faster than any other pricing mistake.

Combined Shipping Strategies

Combined shipping provides win-win opportunities when customers purchase multiple items that can be shipped together in single packages. Sellers save money on packaging materials and postage while reducing time spent on individual shipments. Buyers pay lower total shipping costs that encourage additional purchases.

eBay's checkout system automatically detects when customers buy multiple items from the same seller and prompts for shipping combination options. Smart sellers set up combined shipping rules that offer progressive discounts: full shipping on the first item, reduced rates on additional items. This strategy increases average order values while providing genuine cost savings that justify the discounts through operational efficiencies.

Media Rate Shipping Guidelines

Media Mail offers the cheapest shipping option for books, CDs, DVDs, and other qualifying educational materials, but strict postal service rules create violations that result in package inspection and additional charges. Only genuine educational content qualifies for media rates. Magazines and comic books containing advertisements are excluded regardless of age or content value.

> ▲ **Caution:** Don't abuse Media Mail rates by shipping non-qualifying items. Postal inspections can create expensive problems for your buyers and damage your seller reputation.

The postal service reserves the right to open media mail packages for inspection, and violations result in collecting the difference between media rate and standard postage from recipients. Sellers who abuse media mail risk customer complaints and postal service penalties that damage business relationships. When in doubt, use standard shipping rates instead of risking violations that create expensive problems for buyers who receive unexpected postage due charges.

Postal Insurance Guidelines

Postal insurance rarely provides good value for routine eBay shipments because insurance costs often exceed the protection value for lower-priced items that usually arrive safely. Most packages reach their destinations without damage, making insurance an expensive protection against unlikely events that cost more than occasional losses.

Insurance makes sense only for items worth several hundred dollars or more where replacement costs justify insurance premiums. For routine items under $50, self-insurance through building occasional losses into pricing provides better economics than purchasing insurance that costs more than the statistical loss rate for careful packaging and reliable shipping methods.

International Shipping Program

eBay's Global Shipping Program eliminates the complexity and risk of international sales by enabling sellers to ship domestically while eBay handles international delivery, customs documentation, and import duties. Sellers ship products to eBay's domestic facility, which then manages international shipping and customs compliance that previously required specialized knowledge and paperwork.

This program opens international markets without requiring sellers to understand foreign customs regulations, calculate international shipping rates, or deal with lost packages in foreign postal systems. The service costs more than direct international shipping but provides liability protection and operational simplicity that makes global selling accessible to sellers who lack international shipping expertise.

Free Shipping Strategy Implications

Free shipping has become a search ranking factor that forces sellers to build shipping costs into item prices, fundamentally changing pricing strategies and profit margin calculations. eBay's algorithm favors listings with free shipping, making it nearly impossible to compete effectively while charging separate shipping fees.

> ◆ **Personal Experience**: When I started, I made the rookie mistake of offering "free shipping" on everything. I thought it would make my items more attractive. What I discovered was brutal - I was essentially working for pocket change because I'd forgotten that "free" shipping just means you're eating the cost yourself. Since then, I've always charged actual shipping costs. It keeps the transaction honest and my profit margins intact.

Folding shipping costs into item prices works mathematically but creates psychological barriers for buyers who can't easily compare total costs across different pricing structures. A $25 item with $5 shipping competes against a $30 item with free shipping, but buyers often perceive the free shipping option as better value despite identical total costs.

The free shipping requirement becomes problematic when selling heavy or bulky items where shipping costs vary dramatically by destination. A piece of furniture might cost $50 to ship locally but $200 to ship cross-country, making national free shipping impossible without absurd pricing that kills local sales.

International sales complicate free shipping strategies because cross-border shipping costs often exceed item values for lower-priced products. Offering free domestic shipping while charging international shipping fees creates policy inconsistencies that confuse buyers and complicate listing management.

Package Tracking and Insurance

Ship with tracking on everything. Without it you cannot prove delivery, and without proof of delivery you will lose every "item not received" dispute eBay handles. This is not optional — it's the one absolute in eBay selling that hasn't changed since the platform started.

Carrier insurance sounds protective but is full of exclusions. Electronics, fragile items, and improperly packed goods frequently get denied even when you paid for coverage. For high-value items, photograph the packed box before it leaves your hands. That documentation matters more than the insurance certificate.

Signature confirmation makes sense for items over $750 — that's eBay's threshold for requiring it to maintain seller protection on high-value claims. Below that, it adds cost and friction for buyers who aren't home during delivery windows. Use it when it matters; skip it when it doesn't.

◆ **Personal Experience**: Always, without fail, ship with tracking. The only exception I've made is shipping stamps via first-class mail since tracking isn't available and they only sold for a dollar or two each - not worth the cost of upgrading to a trackable service. But for everything else, tracking is non-negotiable. If you have a tracking number, eBay will almost always side with you in disputes. Without tracking, you're basically guaranteed to lose when buyers claim items never arrived.

Photograph the packed box before it ships — lid closed, address label visible, packing clearly shown. This takes fifteen seconds and is the evidence that resolves damage disputes and fraud claims. Without it you're arguing against a buyer's word with nothing to show.

■ **Danger Zone:** Shipping high-value items without adequate tracking and insurance protection exposes you to total loss when problems occur.

Returns And Refund Processing

eBay's managed returns system automatically processes many return requests without requiring seller approval, fundamentally changing how returns affect cash flow and inventory management. Buyers can often print return labels and ship items back before sellers know returns have been initiated.

eBay's return automation moves fast. Buyers can often generate return labels and ship before you know the return exists. Build return processing into your weekly routine rather than waiting for the notification to surprise you — the faster you inspect and process, the less metric damage the return creates.

Partial refunds for returned items with undisclosed damage or missing components require careful documentation and evidence that eBay's dispute resolution systems often ignore in favor of buyer-friendly policies. Fighting invalid return claims consumes time and effort while rarely producing favorable outcomes for sellers.

Restocking fees and return shipping charges become difficult to collect even when your policies clearly state these requirements. eBay's buyer-friendly policies override seller return terms in many situations, making it hard to recover the actual costs of processing returns.

International Shipping Complexity

International customs forms require accurate values and honest descriptions. Buyers sometimes ask you to under-declare value to reduce their import duties. Don't do it. Customs fraud is a federal offense and the obligation is entirely yours, not the buyer's.

Currency conversion through eBay's managed payments system uses exchange rates that include spreads favoring the platform over sellers. The automatic conversion happens at sale time based on rates you can't control, creating potential profit margin erosion on international transactions.

Prohibited items restrictions vary by destination country and change frequently based on trade regulations and carrier policies. Items legal to ship domestically might violate import restrictions in other countries, creating liability and package seizure risks for uninformed sellers.

The Global Shipping Program simplifies international logistics by having eBay handle customs and international delivery, but the service adds costs that make your items less competitive while removing your control over the international shipping experience. Buyer complaints about GSP delivery issues still affect your seller metrics despite the service being eBay's responsibility.

Packaging And Presentation

Professional packaging affects buyer perception of value and your brand reputation, but packaging costs and time requirements can eliminate profit margins on lower-priced items. The balance between protective packaging and cost control becomes more critical as shipping volume increases.

Branded packaging creates marketing opportunities and professional appearance but requires minimum order quantities and upfront investments that might not be justified for new sellers testing different product categories. Generic packaging works functionally but misses opportunities to build brand recognition and repeat business.

Eco-friendly packaging appeals to environmentally conscious buyers but often costs more and offers less protection than traditional materials. The sustainability message might attract certain buyers while the higher costs reduce profit margins on price-sensitive products.

Package theft prevention requires shipping to secure locations or using services that confirm delivery to actual recipients, but these protections add costs and complexity while not being fully effective against determined thieves. Seller liability for stolen packages varies by shipping method and insurance coverage.

Payments and shipping are the mechanics that make every sale actually happen. Get them wrong and it doesn't matter how good your listings are. Get them right and they become invisible — which is exactly what you want. The goal is a process that runs reliably without requiring your constant attention.

When I first started selling on eBay, I estimated package weights by picking them up and guessing. After several months of this primitive method, I asked a postal employee to weigh one of my boxes and discovered I'd been overestimating by 2 pounds, which meant I was paying as much as a dollar extra per shipment.

A $40 postal scale from Amazon solved this problem immediately and saved far more than its cost within the first few months. The scale paid for itself through accurate shipping calculations that eliminated the overcharges I'd been absorbing through weight guesswork.

This experience taught me that basic equipment investments often provide immediate returns through operational improvements that add up to significant savings over time.

A successful eBay business needs more equipment than optimistic beginners expect but less than equipment vendors want to sell you. The challenge lies in distinguishing between tools that genuinely improve operations and expensive gadgets that promise miraculous results while delivering marginal benefits.

Most new sellers make one of two mistakes: they try to operate without basic equipment and lose money to inefficiency, or they over-invest in premium tools before understanding what they actually need. Start with what solves a real problem you already have. Add more as the business shows you what it needs next.

Essential Measuring and Shipping Equipment

A postal scale represents the single most important equipment purchase for eBay sellers who ship anything heavier than a greeting card. Guessing package weights inevitably leads to overcharging customers or absorbing unexpected shipping costs that destroy profit margins.

Digital postal scales that handle packages up to 30 pounds cost around $40 and save their purchase price within weeks through accurate shipping calculations. Many sellers discover they've been overestimating weights by 1-2 pounds per package, which translates to $50-100 monthly savings for moderate volume operations.

Scale accuracy matters more than fancy features. Basic digital models that display weights in ounces and pounds work perfectly for eBay shipping without expensive bells and whistles that add cost without improving functionality.

Measuring tools complement postal scales by enabling accurate dimension calculations for shipping cost estimates and box selection. A basic tape measure and small ruler handle most measurement needs without requiring expensive precision instruments.

Photography Equipment for Professional Listings

Camera quality directly impacts sales success, but expensive professional equipment often provides marginal improvements over more affordable alternatives that deliver excellent results for eBay purposes.

Smartphones have largely replaced dedicated cameras for eBay photography, and for most sellers that's completely fine. A recent iPhone or Android flagship takes excellent product photos when used correctly. The real advantage of a dedicated camera is consistency — a camera on a tripod stays in one place, uses the same settings, and produces uniform results across a batch of items. If you're shooting ten items in a session, that repeatability matters more than raw image quality.

If you do buy a dedicated camera, you don't need to spend much. A $100-150 point-and-shoot with manual mode and tripod capability handles everything eBay photography requires. The expensive professional gear adds complexity without proportional benefit for product shots. What matters is lighting and consistency, not megapixels.

Tripods eliminate the camera shake and inconsistent angles that plague handheld photography while enabling repeatable photo setups that maintain consistency across multiple listings. Small tabletop tripods work well for most eBay products without requiring expensive full-size equipment.

Memory cards with adequate capacity prevent the frustration of running out of storage during photo sessions while providing backup options when primary cards fail or get misplaced during busy periods.

Lighting Solutions for Quality Photos

Proper lighting transforms amateur photos into professional presentations that increase buyer confidence and sale prices, making lighting equipment one of the best investments for serious eBay sellers.

Desktop lighting kits with adjustable LED panels cost around $40 and eliminate the harsh shadows and color distortion that plague photos taken with camera flashes or inadequate room lighting.

Light tents create professional backgrounds while diffusing light evenly across products to eliminate shadows and reflections that distract from merchandise presentation. Small light tents suitable for most eBay products cost $20-30 and fold flat for storage.

Background materials enable clean, distraction-free photos that focus buyer attention on products instead of cluttered surroundings that suggest unprofessional operations. White and colored fabric backgrounds work better than expensive photographic papers for most eBay applications.

Natural lighting provides excellent results when available, but relying on sunlight creates scheduling constraints and inconsistent conditions that complicate photography workflows during busy selling periods.

★ Pro Tip: Invest in lighting before upgrading cameras. Good lighting with a basic camera produces better results than expensive cameras with poor lighting conditions.

Barcode Readers for Efficient Listing

USB barcode scanners simplify listing creation for books, movies, video games, and other products with UPC or ISBN codes by automatically populating product information and categories.

Inexpensive barcode readers cost around $20 and save substantial time when listing media products that eBay recognizes through its product catalog system. Scanning codes takes seconds compared to manual typing that's prone to errors and time consumption.

Barcode scanning works best for brand-name products in eBay's database but provides limited value for vintage items, collectibles, or products without standardized codes that require manual listing creation.

Scanner compatibility with your computer system matters more than advanced features that add cost without improving basic scanning functionality for eBay applications.

Shipping Supplies and Storage

Shipping supply costs quickly accumulate into significant expenses when purchased retail, making bulk purchasing essential for maintaining profitable operations as sales volume increases.

Padded envelopes work well for books, DVDs, CDs, and other flat items that need protection during shipping. Buying these individually from office stores costs $1-2 each, while bulk purchases reduce costs to $0.25-0.50 per envelope.

Boxes in various sizes handle larger items and provide better protection than envelopes for fragile or valuable merchandise. Standard box sizes work for most eBay products without requiring custom packaging that increases costs and complexity.

Packing materials like bubble wrap, packing peanuts, and air pillows protect merchandise during shipping while demonstrating professional packaging that encourages positive feedback and repeat customers.

Shipping tape secures packages reliably without requiring expensive branded options that add costs without improving functionality. Basic shipping tape works perfectly for eBay applications when applied properly.

Label printing capabilities enable professional shipping labels that improve delivery reliability while providing tracking integration with eBay systems. Basic label printers cost $100-150 and pay for themselves through improved efficiency.

Storage and Organization Solutions

Once your inventory fills more than a shelf or two, organization stops being optional. Items you can't find don't ship on time. Items stored badly get damaged. The system doesn't need to be elaborate — consistent location coding, clear bins, and a dedicated packing area will handle most eBay operations at any reasonable volume. If something valuable is sitting in a space with extreme temperature swings or humidity, move it. That's the whole storage section.

> ▲ **Caution:** Don't over-invest in storage solutions before understanding your actual space and organization needs. Start simple and expand based on real requirements.

Technology Infrastructure

You need a computer that can handle photo editing and browser tabs without freezing, fast enough internet that uploading listing photos isn't a ten-minute event, and a printer for shipping labels. That's the technology infrastructure for most eBay operations. A label printer pays for itself fast in time saved. Everything else — inventory software, photo editing tools, listing managers — buy when a specific problem makes you realize you need it, not before.

Cost-Benefit Analysis for Equipment Purchases

Buy equipment when a real problem makes you need it. A scale saves you money immediately. Basic lighting pays for itself in better photos. Used equipment works fine for almost everything eBay requires. The mistake isn't under-buying — it's spending on gear before you know whether you'll sell enough to justify it.

> ■ **Danger Zone:** Avoid equipment purchases that promise to "revolutionize" your business. Focus on tools that solve specific problems you're actually experiencing.

Maintenance and Replacement Planning

Equipment breaks. That's the whole maintenance section. Clean your scale periodically so the contacts stay accurate. Keep your label printer stocked. Replace batteries in your barcode scanner before they die mid-session. Most equipment issues are caused by deferred basic care, not component failure.

Budget for replacements before you need them rather than after something fails during a busy week. A scale that dies in November during your holiday selling push costs you more in disruption than the $40 it would have cost to replace it in September. Keep one spare label roll and a backup scale if you're doing serious volume. For everything else, know what you'd do if it stopped working today.

The scale, the lighting, the organized shelves — these are tools that make the work easier. They don't make the business. What makes the business is finding things worth selling, describing them honestly, and shipping them on time. Everything else is support infrastructure. Keep it proportionate to what you actually need today, and add to it when the work clearly calls for it.

PART II: Building Your Business

Chapter 7: Product Research and Sourcing

I sold an original Dungeons & Dragons game that had been sitting on my shelf for over forty years. Even though it looked worn from age, it sold on eBay for $400 because collectors value rare items regardless of cosmetic condition when the content remains complete.

The same principle applied to first edition books and animation cells that commanded hundreds of dollars despite showing their age. These items taught me that collectible value often trumps cosmetic condition when rarity and completeness matter more to buyers than pristine appearance.

This experience showed me the importance of researching potential value before dismissing items that look worn or outdated, since collector markets often operate by different value criteria than retail markets.

Finding profitable products to sell on eBay used to be as simple as cleaning out your closets and garage. Every household had decades of accumulated stuff, and the auction format let you test market demand without committing to a price. That casual approach still works occasionally — but building a reliable income from it requires something more deliberate now.

The shift from casual selling to professional sourcing reflects eBay's evolution from a quirky community marketplace into a corporate platform optimized for high-volume sellers. Modern eBay rewards sellers who can consistently find and flip products at scale, not people selling their grandmother's china collection one piece at a time. Understanding how to research profitable products and establish reliable sourcing channels has become essential for anyone who wants to build a sustainable eBay business.

Understanding Market Demand Signals

eBay provides more market intelligence than most sellers ever bother to use. The sold listings feature shows you exactly what buyers pay for specific items, not just what sellers hope to receive. This data reveals the difference between wishful thinking and market reality, but you need to analyze it intelligently to extract useful insights.

Sold listings tell stories about demand patterns, seasonal fluctuations, condition premiums, and price variations that can guide your sourcing decisions. A vintage camera that consistently sells for $200 in working condition but only $50 when broken for parts reveals a restoration opportunity. Items with wide price spreads between different conditions or sellers suggest market inefficiencies you can exploit.

Completed auctions show demand intensity through bidding patterns and final sale prices. Multiple bidders driving prices above Buy It Now levels indicate strong demand and potential for competitive pricing. Single-bidder auctions ending at starting prices suggest weak demand or poor timing that you should avoid replicating.

> ★ **Pro Tip:** Look for items with consistent sell-through rates and stable pricing over 60-90 days. Volatile pricing usually means you're looking at a fad or manipulated market.

Category Analysis for Opportunity Identification

Different eBay categories operate with distinct dynamics that affect profitability and competition levels. Electronics move quickly but have narrow margins and high return rates. Collectibles offer better margins but require specialized knowledge and patience to find buyers. Fashion items turn over fast but deal with sizing issues and seasonal demand shifts.

Category research reveals competition density, average selling prices, and buyer behavior patterns that influence your success potential. Oversaturated categories with hundreds of identical listings make it nearly impossible for new sellers to gain visibility. Niche categories with fewer listings but consistent sales offer better opportunities for sellers willing to develop expertise.

Fee structures vary significantly across categories — some have lower final value fees that improve margins, others face higher fees that require volume to stay profitable. Check the fee schedule for your category before assuming your margins will hold up. A product that works in one category can be a money-loser in another purely because of fee differences.

▲ **Caution:** Avoid categories with complex regulations, authentication requirements, or high fraud risks unless you have specific expertise and can handle the compliance burden.

Sourcing From Retail Arbitrage

Retail arbitrage involves buying discounted merchandise from retail stores and reselling it on eBay for profit. This strategy works best with clearance items, seasonal merchandise, and products with regional price variations that create opportunities for geographic arbitrage.

The key to successful retail arbitrage lies in understanding retail cycles and clearance patterns. Department stores clear seasonal merchandise at predictable times. Electronics retailers dump older model inventory when new versions launch. Toy stores discount items after holiday seasons when demand drops but collectors still want specific items.

Mobile apps that scan barcodes and show current eBay pricing make retail arbitrage more efficient, but they've also increased competition as more sellers use the same tools. Success now requires moving beyond obvious opportunities to find items that other sellers miss or dismiss as unprofitable.

Good relationships with retail employees can get you advance notice of clearance events and better access to discounted inventory. Store managers often prefer selling large quantities to a single buyer who removes merchandise quickly rather than dealing with small individual sales over extended periods.

Online Sourcing Strategies

The internet has democratized access to wholesale sources and international suppliers, but it's also made sourcing more competitive as geographic barriers disappeared. Successful online sourcing requires finding suppliers that other sellers haven't discovered or developing exclusive relationships that provide competitive advantages.

Liquidation websites offer bulk merchandise from store closures, overstock situations, and customer returns. These sources can provide excellent margins but require careful evaluation of condition, demand, and logistics costs that can quickly erode profits if you're not careful.

International sourcing through platforms like Alibaba can provide excellent margins on private label products, but it requires understanding import regulations, quality control, and inventory management that many casual sellers underestimate. The lead times and minimum order quantities also require more capital and planning than domestic sourcing.

> ■ **Danger Zone:** Never source products that require FDA approval, safety certifications, or regulatory compliance unless you fully understand the legal requirements and liability implications.

Estate Sale and Auction Opportunities

Estate sales and local auctions still offer opportunities to find valuable items at below-market prices, but success requires developing expertise in specific categories and understanding local market dynamics. The best opportunities often come from sales that other dealers overlook or don't understand.

Estate sale success depends on arriving early, bringing cash, and knowing what to look for in categories that interest you. Sellers who understand vintage electronics, designer clothing, or collectible categories can spot valuable items that general dealers miss. Building relationships with estate sale companies can provide advance access to sales and better information about inventory.

Online estate sale platforms have expanded access to sales nationwide, but they've also increased competition and shipping costs that affect profitability. Local sales still offer the best opportunities for finding underpriced items because the buyer pool is smaller and more geographically limited.

Thrift Store and Garage Sale Sourcing

Thrift stores and garage sales represent the classic eBay sourcing approach, but success now requires more sophistication than it used to. The best items get picked over quickly by experienced sellers, so you need to develop strategies for finding overlooked opportunities.

Thrift store sourcing works best when you focus on specific categories where you can develop expertise and spot valuable items that other shoppers miss. Understanding brand names, model numbers, and condition factors helps you quickly evaluate potential purchases without spending hours researching every item.

Garage sale success comes from understanding seller psychology and timing your visits strategically. Early morning shoppers get first pick of inventory, but late-day visitors often find sellers willing to negotiate aggressively to avoid packing items back up.

Wholesale and Distributor Relationships

Wholesale sourcing provides the scalability and predictable inventory flow that serious eBay sellers need, but accessing legitimate wholesale sources requires business credentials and often significant minimum orders. Many supposed wholesale directories are actually dropshipping schemes or outdated contact lists that don't provide real value.

Distributor relationships require demonstrating that you can move inventory consistently and handle the administrative requirements of wholesale purchasing. Distributors prefer working with sellers who understand order minimums, payment terms, and return policies that protect their interests.

Regional distributors often provide better opportunities than national companies because they have smaller customer bases and more flexibility in their policies. Local trade shows and industry events can provide access to distributors who don't actively seek eBay sellers but will work with professional buyers.

Product Validation and Testing

Testing products on a small scale before committing to large inventory purchases helps minimize losses from sourcing mistakes and market misjudgments. Starting with single items or small quantities lets you understand demand patterns, return rates, and competition levels without risking significant capital.

eBay's Best Offer feature provides market feedback on pricing that helps validate demand at different price points. Multiple offers on items suggest strong demand that can support higher volumes, while lack of interest indicates you should look for different products or better sourcing prices.

Seasonal testing helps identify products with consistent year-round demand versus items that only sell during specific periods. Knowing seasonality patterns helps you time purchases and avoid getting stuck with inventory that won't move for months.

Building Inventory Management Systems

Successful product sourcing requires systems for tracking costs, managing inventory, and monitoring profitability across different product lines. Manual tracking works for casual selling but becomes unmanageable as your business grows beyond a few dozen items.

Cost tracking needs to include not just purchase prices but also shipping, storage, listing fees, and your time investment to get accurate profitability calculations. Many sellers underestimate the true cost of their inventory and price items below break-even without realizing it.

Inventory rotation becomes crucial as your product volume increases. Items that sit for months tie up capital and storage space while generating ongoing holding costs. Developing systems for identifying and liquidating slow-moving inventory helps maintain cash flow and storage efficiency.

The magic of finding amazing deals still exists. It just requires more work than it used to. The sourcing skills, the market knowledge, the patience to wait for the right inventory — these are what keep working sellers in business. They're learnable, and they compound. Every category you get to know well makes the next one faster to figure out.

eBay photography used to be forgiving. Blurry shots under kitchen fluorescents, a vague description, and buyers bid anyway because the platform ran on goodwill and low expectations. That tolerance is gone. Your photos now compete directly against professional product photography from major retailers, and buyers who don't like what they see scroll past in under a second.

Lighting Fundamentals That Actually Matter

Natural light remains the gold standard for eBay photography because it renders colors accurately and creates even illumination that artificial lighting can't match. Window light provides the soft, diffused illumination that makes products look appealing without harsh shadows or color casts that make even quality items look cheap.

The direction and quality of natural light changes throughout the day, affecting how your photos look and how much editing they need afterward. Morning light tends to be cooler and softer, while afternoon light becomes warmer and more intense. Overcast days provide beautifully even lighting that eliminates harsh shadows, while direct sunlight creates contrast problems that are difficult to fix.

Position your items perpendicular to windows to get even side lighting that reveals texture and detail without creating unwanted shadows. Shooting directly toward or away from windows creates exposure problems that make items look washed out or too dark. The goal is finding the sweet spot where natural light illuminates your item evenly without creating distracting highlights or shadows.

> ★ **Pro Tip:** Use a large white poster board as a reflector to bounce light into shadow areas and create more even illumination without additional light sources.

Background Selection Strategy

Your background choice affects perceived value more than most sellers realize. Clean, neutral backgrounds help items stand out and look professional, while cluttered or distracting backgrounds make even expensive items look cheap. The background should disappear, letting buyers focus entirely on the item you're selling.

White backgrounds work well for most items because they look clean, photograph easily, and provide good contrast for product details. Colored backgrounds can work but require more careful color coordination to avoid clashing with your items or creating color casts that affect how buyers perceive the actual product colors.

Textured backgrounds like fabric or wood can add visual interest but often distract from the item and create focus problems in photos. Simple is almost always better than complex backgrounds that help rather than hinder sales.

Lifestyle backgrounds that show items in use can help buyers visualize ownership, but they require more careful composition and styling to look natural rather than staged. Most eBay sellers lack the styling skills to make lifestyle shots work effectively, so neutral backgrounds provide better results with less effort.

Composition Techniques For Mobile Optimization

Mobile shoppers view your photos on screens smaller than playing cards, which means composition rules that worked for desktop viewing no longer apply. Details that were clearly visible on large monitors become invisible on phone screens, and busy compositions that looked fine on desktops become cluttered messes on mobile devices.

Fill the frame with your item to maximize the detail visible in thumbnail images. Empty space that looks professional on desktop monitors becomes wasted screen real estate on mobile devices where every pixel matters for showing product details that influence purchase decisions.

Shoot from angles that show the most important features and details clearly. Front-facing shots work well for items with obvious fronts, while three-quarter angles often provide better perspective for three-dimensional objects. The key is choosing angles that communicate what the item is and its condition quickly.

Multiple photos should tell a complete story about your item without requiring buyers to zoom in on every image to understand what they're buying. Wide shots establish context, medium shots show important details, and close-ups reveal condition and quality factors that affect value.

> ▲ **Caution:** Keep critical details away from photo edges. eBay's mobile app crops images to fit various screen layouts, and anything near the edge of the frame risks being cut off when buyers view in search results or on smaller screens.

Technical Photography Settings

Most modern smartphones take excellent photos when you understand how to use their camera features effectively. Auto mode works fine for basic shots, but understanding manual controls helps you get better results in challenging lighting conditions or with difficult subjects.

Focus control becomes crucial when photographing small items or details that automatic focus systems might miss. Tap your phone screen where you want sharp focus, and the camera will adjust exposure and focus for that specific area. This simple technique dramatically improves photo quality for detail shots and close-ups.

Exposure compensation helps balance lighting when auto mode produces photos that are too bright or too dark. Most camera apps let you adjust exposure by tapping and dragging up or down on the screen. Slightly underexposing photos often produces better results than overexposing because you can brighten dark photos more easily than you can recover blown-out highlights.

Grid lines help compose shots using the rule of thirds and keep horizons level. Most camera apps can display grid overlays that help you position items more attractively and avoid tilted photos that look amateurish.

Condition Documentation Strategies

Thorough condition documentation protects you from return disputes while building buyer confidence in your honesty and attention to detail. Buyers prefer dealing with sellers who disclose flaws upfront over those who hide problems that become unpleasant surprises after delivery.

Photograph obvious flaws and damage clearly, but also document subtle wear patterns and condition issues that might not be immediately apparent. Close-up photos of wear areas, scratches, and age-related changes help buyers understand exactly what they're purchasing.

Before and after shots can help illustrate cleaning or restoration work you've done to improve an item's condition. These photos demonstrate the care you've taken and help justify pricing for items you've improved beyond their found condition.

Multiple angles and lighting conditions help reveal details that single photos might miss. What looks perfect under soft lighting might show wear patterns under direct light, and different angles can reveal damage or wear that frontal shots don't capture.

> ■ **Danger Zone:** Never attempt to hide obvious damage with strategic photography or editing. Buyers will discover hidden problems and leave negative feedback that hurts your long-term success.

Photo Editing for eBay Success

Basic photo editing can dramatically improve your listing photos without requiring expensive software or advanced technical skills. Simple adjustments to brightness, contrast, and color balance often transform mediocre photos into compelling sales tools.

Brightness and contrast adjustments help photos look crisp and appealing without making them look obviously edited. Slightly increasing contrast makes photos pop on mobile screens, while brightness adjustments help compensate for lighting conditions that were less than ideal when you took the photos.

Color correction becomes important when indoor lighting creates color casts that make items look different from their actual colors. Buyers want to see accurate colors that help them understand what they're actually purchasing, not artistic interpretations that mislead about actual appearance.

Cropping helps eliminate distracting backgrounds and focuses attention on the item you're selling. Tight crops work well for mobile viewing, but leave some breathing room around your items to avoid photos that feel cramped or claustrophobic.

Title Optimization for Search Visibility

Your listing title carries more weight for search ranking than any other single factor, so every word needs to work hard to attract both eBay's algorithm and potential buyers. The 80-character limit forces brutal prioritization of the most important keywords while maintaining readability.

Brand names, model numbers, and key descriptors should appear early in titles because mobile screens often cut off longer titles. Put the most important information first to make sure it remains visible even when titles get truncated in search results or mobile listings.

Condition indicators help buyers quickly understand what they're looking at and can improve click-through rates when buyers are specifically looking for new, used, or vintage items. Clear condition descriptions in titles save buyers time and help qualify serious prospects.

Size, color, and other specification details help buyers find exactly what they want while filtering out browsers who aren't serious prospects. Specific details attract targeted buyers who know what they want and are ready to purchase when they find it.

Description Writing for Conversion

Your item description needs to work for both search engines and human buyers who are reading on mobile devices. Front-load the most important information because mobile buyers often skim descriptions quickly while scrolling through multiple listings.

Search-friendly writing includes relevant keywords naturally throughout the description without resorting to keyword stuffing that makes listings sound robotic. Write for humans first, then optimize for search engines by including terms that buyers actually use when looking for items like yours.

Technical specifications and detailed measurements help serious buyers evaluate whether your item meets their needs. Include dimensions, weights, model numbers, and compatibility information that helps buyers make informed decisions without needing to ask questions.

Story elements can help create emotional connections with buyers, especially for vintage or collectible items. Brief histories, previous ownership details, or interesting background information can differentiate your listing from identical items offered by other sellers.

Mobile-First Design Principles

Design your listings assuming that most buyers will view them on phones because that's the reality of modern eBay shopping. What looks great on desktop computers often becomes unreadable on mobile devices, so optimize for small screens first.

Short paragraphs and plenty of white space make descriptions easier to read on small screens. Wall-of-text descriptions that worked fine on desktop monitors become intimidating blocks that mobile users skip entirely.

Important information should appear early in descriptions because mobile users often don't scroll through entire listings. Put size, condition, and key features near the top where impatient mobile shoppers will see them immediately.

Photo order becomes crucial for mobile optimization because buyers often make purchase decisions based on the first few images without scrolling through entire photo galleries. Lead with your strongest photos that clearly show what you're selling and its condition.

A/B Testing Listing Performance

Testing different approaches to photography, titles, and descriptions helps identify what works best for your specific items and buyer audience. Small changes in presentation can create significant differences in views, watchers, and final sale prices.

Photo variations let you test whether lifestyle shots, plain backgrounds, or detail close-ups generate better buyer engagement. Try different main photos and track which versions get more views and higher sale prices.

Title experiments help identify which keywords and phrases resonate with buyers in your categories. Test different keyword combinations and descriptive phrases to find combinations that generate more search traffic and higher conversion rates.

Price point testing reveals optimal pricing strategies for different types of items and market conditions. Start with higher prices and gradually reduce them to find the sweet spot where you maximize both sale probability and profit margins.

The goal hasn't changed: show buyers clearly what they're getting and make them want it. The tools to do that are better now than they've ever been. A decent phone, good light, and some attention to composition will take you further than elaborate setups that require expensive gear. What matters is whether the buyer can see the item clearly and trust what they're seeing. Start there.

Pricing items on eBay used to be straightforward: check what similar items sold for, price yours competitively, and let the auction format sort out the rest. The fixed-price marketplace that replaced it works differently. Professional sellers run pricing algorithms. Data tools track real-time competitor moves. And the platform's search algorithm uses your price as a ranking signal — which means getting your pricing wrong affects not just whether buyers purchase, but whether they ever see you at all.

Understanding eBay's Price-Driven Algorithm

eBay's search algorithm favors listings that convert browsers into buyers, and your price is a direct input to that calculation. Items priced significantly above market rates get fewer clicks, lower conversion rates, and reduced search placement that compounds the pricing problem by making overpriced items even less visible.

The algorithm considers not just your current pricing but also your historical pricing patterns and conversion rates when determining search placement. Sellers who consistently price items competitively and achieve good conversion rates earn better search visibility, while sellers with poor conversion history get buried deeper in search results.

Price changes during active listings can trigger algorithm adjustments that affect visibility. Dramatic price reductions often boost search placement temporarily, but frequent price changes can signal desperation that hurts long-term ranking. The algorithm rewards pricing consistency and market understanding over reactive price manipulation.

Competitive pricing within your category affects not just individual item performance but your overall seller metrics that influence all your listings. Sellers who price most items appropriately see better performance across their entire inventory, while sellers who regularly overprice items hurt their account-wide search visibility.

Market Research Techniques That Matter

Sold listings provide the foundation for intelligent pricing decisions, but most sellers analyze this data superficially and miss important patterns that affect pricing strategy. Looking at recent sold prices gives you baseline market value, but understanding the context behind those sales reveals opportunities for better pricing.

Auction ending times and formats affect final sale prices in ways that influence your pricing strategy. Items that end during peak shopping hours often achieve higher prices than identical items ending at odd hours. Understanding these patterns helps you time your listings and price your Buy It Now items competitively.

Condition premiums vary dramatically across categories and price ranges. A mint-condition vintage toy might command triple the price of a good-condition example, while electronics show smaller condition premiums because functionality matters more than cosmetic perfection. Knowing condition premiums in your categories helps you price appropriately and identify restoration opportunities.

Seasonal demand patterns affect pricing strategies and timing decisions. Holiday decorations peak in November and December but become nearly worthless in January. Understanding seasonal cycles helps you price for current demand and avoid getting stuck with inventory during low-demand periods.

> ★ **Pro Tip:** Track sold prices for identical items over 90 days to understand normal price ranges and identify unusual high or low sales that don't represent typical market value.

Psychological Pricing Principles

Psychological pricing effects remain powerful even in eBay's data-driven environment where buyers can easily compare prices across multiple sellers. The difference between $19.99 and $20.00 seems trivial, but buyer behavior data shows these small pricing differences significantly affect click-through rates and conversion.

Charm pricing using prices ending in 9 or 99 increases perceived value and conversion rates across most product categories. Buyers process $99 as significantly cheaper than $100 even though the difference is minimal. This effect works even for sophisticated buyers who understand the psychological manipulation.

Round number pricing can signal quality and premium positioning for higher-end items. A vintage guitar priced at $500 feels more serious and valuable than one priced at $499.99. The psychological effect varies by product category and buyer demographics, so test different approaches to find what works for your items.

Bundle pricing can increase average sale values while making individual item costs less transparent. Selling a camera with lens, case, and accessories as a bundle often generates higher total revenue than selling items separately, even when buyers don't need all components.

Competitive Analysis and Positioning

Knowing your competition means analyzing not just pricing but also seller ratings, shipping costs, return policies, and listing quality that affect buyer choice when multiple sellers offer similar items. Price alone rarely determines buyer decisions when other factors create perceived value differences.

Seller feedback scores and ratings significantly affect buyer willingness to pay premium prices. New sellers often need to price below established competitors to overcome buyer reluctance about dealing with unknown sellers. Building reputation takes time, but it eventually allows higher pricing and better profit margins.

Shipping cost strategies affect total buyer cost and search placement in ways that influence your pricing decisions. Sellers who offer free shipping by building costs into item prices often achieve better search visibility than sellers who charge actual shipping costs, even when total buyer cost is identical.

Geographic factors affect competition and pricing in categories where shipping costs or local pickup options matter. Bulky items that cost significantly more to ship long distances create regional pricing opportunities for sellers in different markets.

> ▲ **Caution:** Don't price match competitors without understanding their business models. Some sellers use loss-leader pricing or volume discounts that aren't sustainable for smaller operations.

Dynamic Pricing Strategies

Static pricing works for some items, but dynamic pricing strategies that adjust to market conditions, competition, and demand patterns often generate better results. The key is systematic approaches based on data rather than emotional reactions to slow sales or competitive pressure.

Starting prices for auction-style listings require balancing search visibility, bidder attraction, and reserve protection. Low starting prices attract more bidders and improve search placement but risk selling valuable items below market value if bidding competition doesn't develop.

Price testing through multiple similar listings helps identify optimal pricing for different items and market conditions. List identical items at different prices to see which approach generates better results, but avoid flooding the market with too many similar listings that compete against each other.

Markdown timing affects both sales velocity and profit margins. Gradual price reductions over time often generate better results than dramatic one-time cuts because they maintain perceived value while responding to market feedback. Steep initial discounts can signal desperation and hurt perceived value.

Category-Specific Pricing Considerations

Different eBay categories operate with distinct pricing dynamics that affect strategy and buyer expectations. Electronics buyers focus heavily on price comparison and technical specifications, while collectibles buyers often pay premiums for condition, rarity, and seller expertise that justify higher margins.

Fashion categories deal with sizing uncertainties and seasonal demand that create pricing challenges and opportunities. Items in standard sizes often command higher prices than unusual sizes, but hard-to-find sizes in popular styles can generate premium pricing for sellers who understand their market.

Collectibles pricing depends heavily on condition, rarity, and market timing that require specialized knowledge to optimize. Pricing collectibles requires understanding grading standards, market trends, and collector preferences that differ dramatically from mainstream retail pricing psychology.

Books and media face intense price competition from major retailers and other volume sellers. Success in these categories often requires focusing on unique editions, out-of-print titles, or items with local interest that command premiums over commodity pricing.

> ■ **Danger Zone:** Never price items below your total costs unless you're specifically liquidating inventory. Many sellers forget to include eBay fees, shipping costs, and time investment when calculating break-even prices.

International Pricing Considerations

Global Shipping Program fees and international buyer behavior affect pricing strategies when you sell internationally. International buyers often accept higher prices because they have fewer local options, but they also deal with longer shipping times and potential customs issues that affect their willingness to pay premiums.

Currency conversion and international payment processing add costs that affect pricing for international sales. Understanding these additional costs helps you price appropriately for global markets without sacrificing profit margins to currency fluctuations or processing fees.

Regional demand patterns are real. Vintage American products, items with US cultural cachet, and specialty goods that are hard to find overseas can command premium prices from international buyers who have no local alternatives. That same item may be worthless in a domestic market saturated with identical listings. If you source with international buyers in mind, you can price accordingly.

Timing and Market Conditions

Market timing affects pricing success more than most sellers realize. Economic conditions, seasonal patterns, and news events can dramatically shift demand and pricing for specific categories in ways that require pricing strategy adjustments.

Holiday seasons create predictable demand patterns that affect pricing strategies and inventory planning. Understanding which items peak during different holidays helps you time purchases and pricing to maximize seasonal demand opportunities.

Economic cycles affect luxury and discretionary spending in ways that influence pricing for non-essential items. During economic uncertainty, buyers become more price-sensitive and focus on value-oriented purchases rather than premium items.

Repricing and Optimization

Successful eBay selling requires ongoing price optimization based on market feedback, competition changes, and performance data. Set-and-forget pricing rarely produces optimal results in eBay's dynamic marketplace where conditions change constantly.

Performance metrics like views, watchers, and conversion rates provide feedback about pricing effectiveness that helps guide adjustments. Items with high views but low conversion rates often indicate pricing problems that prevent browsers from becoming buyers.

Seasonal adjustments help maintain sales velocity as demand patterns change throughout the year. Items that sell quickly in season often require price reductions during off-peak periods to maintain inventory turnover and cash flow.

Pricing on eBay is not a set-and-forget task. The market moves, competitors adjust, seasons shift, and your own cost structure changes. The sellers who price something once and walk away leave money on the table or price themselves out of visibility without knowing why. The ones who check and adjust regularly don't necessarily spend more time on it — they just make it a habit instead of a project.

The sweet spot between what buyers will pay and what you need to make is real, and it's different for every item and every category. You find it by looking at what has actually sold, pricing accordingly, watching what happens, and adjusting. That's the whole system. It's less complicated than it sounds once you stop guessing and start looking at data.

Chapter 10: Managing Inventory and Orders

Inventory management on eBay used to mean keeping a mental note of what you had listed and remembering to ship when something sold. At a dozen items that works. At a hundred it starts breaking down. At several hundred it fails — and when it fails, eBay's algorithm is measuring the fallout in your metrics before you've finished cleaning it up.

The moment your inventory outgrows a notebook, things start falling through the cracks. You oversell an item you thought you had. You ship the wrong thing to the wrong address. You spend twenty minutes hunting for something you know you listed last week. These aren't signs you're a bad seller — they're signs your system hasn't kept up with your business. eBay will punish you for it either way.

Inventory Tracking Systems That Scale

Spreadsheet tracking works fine when you're selling a few dozen items, but it becomes unmanageable and error-prone as your inventory grows. Most sellers discover this limitation the hard way when they oversell items, lose track of costs, or spend hours updating listings manually because their tracking system can't keep up with their business growth.

Professional inventory management software automates the repetitive tasks that consume increasing amounts of time as your business scales. These systems track costs, monitor stock levels, sync across multiple selling platforms, and generate reports that help you understand which products and strategies generate profits.

Cloud-based systems provide access from multiple devices and locations, which becomes crucial when you're sourcing inventory away from your home office or need to update listings while traveling. The ability to check inventory levels and update listings from your phone prevents overselling and missed opportunities when you're not at your computer.

Integration with eBay's API allows real-time synchronization between your inventory system and active listings. When you sell an item, your inventory automatically updates without manual intervention. When you add new inventory, you can create listings directly from your inventory management system without double data entry.

> ★ **Pro Tip:** Start with inventory management software early, even when you think spreadsheets are sufficient. Converting data from manual systems becomes exponentially more difficult as your inventory grows.

Storage and Organization Strategies

Physical inventory organization directly affects your shipping speed and accuracy, both of which influence buyer satisfaction and eBay algorithm ranking. Sellers who can locate and ship items quickly maintain better metrics than sellers who waste time hunting through disorganized storage areas.

Location coding systems help you find items quickly without relying on memory or visual searching. Simple alphanumeric codes that correspond to specific shelves, bins, or storage areas allow you to locate any item within minutes. The investment in labeling and organization pays dividends in reduced shipping time and fewer location-related errors.

Dedicated shipping areas with supplies, scales, and packing materials simplify the fulfillment process and reduce the time between sale and shipment. Professional setups don't require expensive equipment, just organized workspace that eliminates the need to gather supplies for each shipment.

Climate control and security become important considerations as your inventory value increases. Items damaged by humidity, temperature fluctuations, or theft can destroy months of profit in a single incident. Basic environmental controls and security measures protect your investment in inventory.

Order Processing Workflows

Every sale is a promise to ship. The faster and more reliably you fulfill it, the better your metrics, the happier your buyers, and the fewer customer service problems you'll deal with. The sellers who struggle with order processing are usually the ones who treat it as something they get to rather than something they do on a fixed schedule.

Automated payment confirmation triggers immediate order processing without waiting for manual payment checks. eBay's managed payments system eliminates most payment delays, but sellers still need systems that begin fulfillment processes automatically when payments clear.

Printing shipping labels immediately after payment confirmation saves time and reduces errors compared to batching label printing. Most shipping software integrates with eBay to pull order information automatically, eliminating manual data entry that creates opportunities for address errors or shipping mistakes.

Order verification steps prevent costly shipping errors that damage buyer relationships and hurt seller metrics. Simple checklists that confirm item condition, shipping address accuracy, and packaging adequacy catch problems before they become negative feedback or return requests.

> ▲ **Caution:** Never ship items without delivery confirmation, regardless of value. eBay's seller protection requires proof of delivery, and untracked shipments leave you vulnerable to false claims.

Multi-Platform Inventory Synchronization

Selling across multiple platforms increases exposure and sales opportunities but creates inventory management challenges that can lead to overselling and customer service problems. Successful multi-platform sellers use systems that maintain accurate inventory counts across all selling channels.

Real-time inventory synchronization prevents overselling when the same item is listed on eBay, Amazon, Facebook Marketplace, and other platforms simultaneously. When an item sells on one platform, professional systems immediately update or remove listings on all other platforms to prevent double sales.

Platform-specific optimization requires tailoring listings to each platform's requirements and buyer expectations while maintaining consistent inventory tracking. eBay listings might emphasize auction features, while Amazon listings focus on search optimization and Prime eligibility.

Centralized order management consolidates orders from multiple platforms into single workflows that simplify fulfillment regardless of where buyers made their purchases. This approach reduces errors and ensures consistent service levels across all selling channels.

Cost Tracking and Profitability Analysis

Accurate cost tracking becomes crucial as inventory complexity increases and you need to understand which products and strategies generate real profits versus those that just generate revenue. Many sellers discover they're losing money on certain items because they didn't track all associated costs properly.

Total cost calculations must include purchase price, shipping to your location, eBay fees, payment processing fees, shipping to buyers, packaging materials, and your time investment. Sellers who only consider purchase prices often price items below break-even without realizing their mistake until they analyze complete profitability.

Category-level profitability analysis reveals which product types generate the best returns on investment and time spent. Some categories might generate high gross revenue but low net profits due to high fees, return rates, or time requirements that make them unattractive despite strong sales volume.

Seasonal profitability tracking helps optimize inventory timing and purchasing decisions. Items that generate excellent profits during peak seasons might become money losers during slow periods when price competition intensifies and demand drops.

Seasonal Inventory Management

eBay selling has seasons, and if you're not thinking two or three months ahead, you're already behind. The sellers buying Christmas inventory in October are competing against sellers who bought in August. By the time you're listing holiday items in late November, the early buyers have already captured the premium pricing window.

Source seasonal items early, list them early, and price them at the top of the market. As the season progresses and competition piles in, you have room to lower prices while latecomers are already at the floor. That pricing buffer is one of the few advantages that rewards planning over impulse buying.

Know when to cut and run. Halloween costumes don't sell in November. Christmas decor tanks on December 26th. If you're still sitting on seasonal inventory when the season ends, drop the price fast and move it. Holding it for next year ties up cash and storage space for twelve months. The math rarely works out in your favor.

Also account for what seasonal buying does to your storage space. A spare bedroom that works fine for year-round inventory becomes impossible to navigate when you've added sixty boxes of holiday merchandise. Running out of workspace during your busiest selling period is a problem you can see coming from months away — plan for it.

Quality Control and Inspection Processes

Check everything twice: once before you list it, once before you ship it. That sounds obvious, but sellers skip it constantly, especially when they're busy, and then spend twice as long dealing with the returns and disputes that result. A two-minute inspection before listing catches the cracked hinge, the missing battery cover, the stain you somehow missed the first time.

Before listing: check condition against how you plan to describe it. If you're calling it "excellent," make sure it is. Test anything electronic. Verify that sets and collections are complete. Find the problem now, when you can decide whether to fix it, discount it, or pass on the item entirely — not after you've already promised a buyer something you can't deliver.

Before shipping: pull the item, compare it against the listing photos, check for anything that might have happened in storage. Items sitting in bins get bumped, stacked on, and handled. What was fine three weeks ago when you listed it might not be fine now. Catching that before it leaves your hands is always cheaper than dealing with it after.

If the same type of problem keeps showing up — items arriving damaged, descriptions that don't match buyer expectations, missing parts — track it. Recurring issues almost always point back to a specific sourcing problem or a gap in your inspection process. Fix the root cause rather than just apologizing to buyers one at a time.

Automated Listing and Repricing Tools

At some point, manually creating every listing becomes the thing that stops your business from growing. If listing one item takes twenty minutes, listing fifty items takes sixteen hours. That math forces a choice: stay small, or find tools that handle the repetitive parts so you can focus on the decisions that actually require judgment.

Bulk listing tools let you create templates for item types you list repeatedly and push batches of listings at once. If you source twenty similar items from the same estate sale, you're not starting from scratch on each one — you're adjusting a template. The time savings add up fast once you're past a few dozen listings a week.

Repricing tools watch competitor listings and adjust your prices automatically based on rules you set. You define the floor, the minimum price you'll accept, and the tool handles everything above it. This keeps you competitive without requiring you to manually monitor prices on hundreds of items every day.

Some tools analyze your listing performance and flag what's underperforming — items getting clicks but no sales usually have a price problem; items getting no clicks at all usually have a title problem. That kind of systematic feedback is hard to see when you're managing everything manually and harder still to act on without tools that surface it clearly.

Return and Refund Processing

Returns are part of the business. Fighting that reality wastes more energy than just building a clean process for handling them. The goal isn't to eliminate returns — it's to process them fast, protect your metrics, and get returned items back into sellable condition without losing a week of your time on each one.

Have a clear return policy and stick to it. Ambiguity in your policy doesn't protect you — it just creates arguments. Buyers who know exactly what to expect are less likely to escalate to eBay cases. When they do request a return, process it promptly. Dragging it out doesn't improve the outcome and it does hurt your seller standing.

When the item comes back, inspect it immediately. Condition that was fine when it left can change in transit or during the buyer's handling of it. Catch that before the item goes back on the shelf and gets relisted as something it no longer is.

eBay's policies do allow restocking fees and return shipping charges in certain situations. Know what those situations are and use them when they apply. That said, fighting a buyer over $4 in return shipping on a $25 item is rarely worth it. Pick your battles based on the actual money involved, not principle.

None of this is complicated. It just requires doing it consistently instead of handling each situation like it's the first time you've encountered it. The sellers who build clean inventory and order systems early don't spend less time on their business — they spend that time on things that actually grow it.

I accidentally shipped the wrong product to a customer once, grabbing a DVD instead of the video game he'd ordered and putting it in the wrong envelope. After dropping the packages at the post office, I got home and saw the game sitting on my counter, realizing my mistake immediately.

Even though it would be days before the customer knew there was a problem, I sent an email right away admitting the error and telling him to keep the DVD with my compliments. I made it clear that I was shipping the correct game out that same day, which I did. The customer rewarded me with positive feedback and said he wouldn't hesitate to purchase from me again.

This experience taught me that proactive communication about mistakes often prevents problems from escalating into negative feedback situations. Customers appreciate honesty and quick resolution more than perfect execution.

Customer service on eBay used to be proportional. Buyers understood they were dealing with a person, not a fulfillment center, and they gave sellers the benefit of the doubt when things took a few extra days or a photo wasn't perfect. Amazon trained that patience out of them. Now the same buyer who's forgiving in person expects Prime-level logistics from someone working out of a spare bedroom.

The platform's seller rating system turns every customer interaction into a metric. A slow reply, a disputed return, a miscommunication about condition — each one feeds into your standing in ways that affect search visibility long after the transaction is closed. Getting customer service right isn't just about keeping buyers happy. It's about protecting the account health those buyers are measuring you on.

Understanding Modern Buyer Expectations

Today's eBay buyers arrive with expectations shaped by Amazon Prime, social media customer service, and a broader culture of instant gratification that treats any delay or inconvenience as unacceptable service failure. They expect immediate responses to questions, same-day shipping, and hassle-free returns regardless of whether they're buying from a billion-dollar corporation or someone selling collectibles as a side business.

◆ **Personal Experience:** I had one local buyer who became my best customer over the course of a year. He started by buying a single model kit, then kept coming back for more. Eventually he was buying over a hundred kits annually, often messaging me about what he was looking for before I even listed new inventory. We worked out bulk pricing discounts and free pickup since he lived nearby - he got better deals, I saved on shipping costs and eBay fees, and we both benefited from the relationship. That single customer probably generated more profit than dozens of one-time buyers.

The expectation gap between what buyers demand and what individual sellers can realistically provide creates constant tension that requires careful management. You can't compete with Amazon's logistics network, but you can provide personal attention and expertise that large retailers can't match. The key is setting realistic expectations while delivering consistently excellent service within your actual capabilities.

Communication speed has become a competitive advantage that affects both buyer satisfaction and eBay's algorithm ranking. Buyers who receive quick, helpful responses are more likely to complete purchases and leave positive feedback. eBay's search algorithm considers response time as a ranking factor, so slow communication hurts both individual transactions and overall account performance.

The tone and clarity of your messages matters more than most sellers realize. A well-phrased response to a frustrated buyer can defuse the situation before it becomes a case. A defensive or dismissive reply to the same message escalates it. You're not just answering a question — you're managing a relationship that will end in either positive feedback or a dispute, and your message often determines which.

> ★ **Pro Tip:** Create template responses for common questions, but personalize each message with specific details about the buyer's inquiry to avoid sounding robotic.

Proactive Communication Strategies

Proactive communication prevents problems before they develop into customer service issues that require time-consuming resolution. Sellers who anticipate buyer concerns and address them preemptively spend less time managing complaints and disputes than sellers who only respond to problems after they occur.

Shipping notifications with tracking information reduce anxiety and prevent "where is my item" messages that consume time without generating revenue. Automated systems can send these notifications immediately when you create shipping labels, eliminating the need for manual communication while keeping buyers informed about their order status.

Delivery confirmation messages help make sure buyers know their items have arrived and encourage them to leave feedback while their purchase experience is fresh in their minds. These messages also provide opportunities to address any immediate concerns before they escalate into return requests or negative feedback.

Condition clarifications in your initial communications help set accurate expectations for items with condition issues or unique characteristics that might not be obvious from photos. Taking time to explain condition details upfront prevents misunderstandings that lead to returns and disputes.

Handling Inquiries and Questions

Buyer inquiries often reveal opportunities to provide additional information that helps close sales and prevents future problems. Professional sellers view questions as sales opportunities rather than interruptions, using inquiries to demonstrate expertise and build buyer confidence.

Knowing what you're selling matters when buyers ask technical questions about compatibility, sizing, or usage. A seller who can answer confidently and accurately builds the kind of trust that converts browsers into buyers and turns one-time purchases into repeat customers. Sellers who clearly don't know their own inventory don't earn that trust — and often don't earn the sale either.

Response timing affects both individual sales and overall account metrics that influence search ranking. eBay tracks message response times and uses this data as a seller performance metric. Fast responses improve your standing with both buyers and the algorithm that determines listing visibility.

Detailed answers that address not just the specific question but related concerns demonstrate professionalism and expertise that builds buyer confidence. Comprehensive responses often prevent follow-up questions while providing information that helps buyers feel confident about their purchase decisions.

> ▲ **Caution:** Never promise shipping speeds, delivery dates, or product performance that you can't guarantee. Overpromising leads to disappointed buyers and negative feedback.

Managing Returns and Exchanges

Returns will happen. Fighting that reality costs more than building a clean, fast process for handling them. The goal is to process returns quickly, recover what value you can, and move on without letting the emotional friction of being returned to affect how long it takes.

Return authorization processes help make sure buyers follow proper procedures that protect your interests while providing clear guidance about return requirements. Structured return procedures reduce confusion and disputes that can escalate into negative feedback or eBay cases.

Condition evaluation of returned items determines whether you can resell them at full price, need to adjust pricing for condition changes, or should remove them from inventory entirely. Systematic evaluation prevents listing items with undisclosed damage that creates future customer service problems.

Restocking procedures help returned items get back into sellable inventory quickly when they're in resellable condition. Efficient restocking minimizes the time items spend out of inventory and helps maintain cash flow from returned merchandise.

Cost recovery strategies help minimize the financial impact of returns through legitimate restocking fees, return shipping charges, and partial refunds that reflect actual condition or usage. Understanding eBay's policies around these charges helps you recover costs while maintaining compliance.

Dealing with Difficult Buyers

Difficult buyers show up on every eBay account. What separates sellers who handle them well from those who burn out on them is having clear policies, maintaining composure when pushed, and knowing the difference between a legitimate complaint worth addressing and an attempt to extract something for nothing.

Unreasonable demands often stem from buyer misunderstandings about eBay policies, shipping limitations, or product characteristics that can be resolved through patient education. Taking time to explain policies and limitations often converts difficult situations into positive buyer relationships.

Escalation prevention requires recognizing when buyer concerns are legitimate versus when they're attempting to manipulate the system for undeserved concessions.

Professional sellers learn to distinguish between genuine problems that deserve accommodation and manipulation attempts that require firm boundaries.

Documentation becomes crucial when dealing with problematic buyers who might file eBay cases or leave retaliatory feedback. Maintaining records of all communications and actions taken helps protect you in disputes while demonstrating professional handling of customer service issues.

> ■ **Danger Zone:** Never engage in arguments or emotional responses with difficult buyers. Professional communication protects you legally and helps maintain your seller standing.

Building Long-Term Customer Relationships

Most eBay buyers are one-time transactions and that's fine. But the buyers who come back are worth ten times what a first-time buyer is worth, and most sellers never put any effort into keeping them. They ship the item, wait for feedback, and move on. That's leaving money on the table.

eBay makes repeat customer relationships harder than they should be — you can't email your buyers, you can't run a mailing list, the platform actively discourages off-platform contact. What you can do is follow up inside eBay's messaging system after delivery, thank buyers, and let them know what else you have. It's low-tech and it works better than most sellers expect.

Pay attention to what repeat buyers purchase. If someone has bought vintage electronics from you three times, they're a collector. When you list something new in that category, reach out. A personal message that says "I just listed something I think you'd be interested in" costs you thirty seconds and occasionally turns into a sale you wouldn't have made otherwise.

Feedback follows service. Buyers who feel they got a good deal and were treated well leave positive feedback without being asked. Buyers who had a mediocre experience leave nothing, or worse. You can't manufacture good feedback — you earn it by doing the basics right every time.

Feedback Management Strategies

eBay's feedback system is unforgiving in a specific way: one negative can undo dozens of positives in a buyer's eyes. The percentage looks fine, but buyers read the actual comments. A single "item not as described" sitting on your profile costs you sales you'll never know you lost.

Send a brief message when tracking shows delivery. Not a request for feedback, eBay frowns on explicit solicitation, just a confirmation that that the item arrived and an invitation to reach out with any questions. It keeps the transaction feeling personal and reminds the buyer to leave feedback while the experience is fresh.

Most negative feedback can be avoided by getting ahead of problems. If you know shipping will be delayed, message the buyer before they have to ask. If an item arrives damaged, contact them first. Buyers are much more forgiving when you acknowledge the problem than when they have to chase you down.

When you do get a negative, respond to it publicly and professionally. You're not writing for the buyer who left it — that relationship is over. You're writing for every future buyer who reads it. A calm, factual response that shows you handled the situation like an adult does more good than the negative does damage.

Service Recovery Techniques

Things go wrong. Items get lost in transit. Packages arrive damaged. You ship the wrong size. The question isn't whether problems will happen — it's how fast you deal with them and whether the buyer ends up feeling taken care of or abandoned.

Figure out what actually went wrong before you respond. Not so you can defend yourself — so you can fix it properly. A buyer who gets a damaged item doesn't want an explanation about how the post office handled it. They want to know what you're going to do about it. Lead with the solution, not the excuse.

Be fair with compensation but don't be a pushover. A full refund on a legitimately damaged item is the right call. A full refund because someone changed their mind and is trying to avoid paying return shipping is not. Know the difference and hold the line on the second type — eBay's policies actually give you room to do that.

After you resolve something, check back in. A short message a few days later asking if everything arrived okay and if they're happy costs you nothing. Most buyers are surprised by it, in a good way. The ones who had a bad experience and got it fixed right are often your most loyal customers afterward — they know you'll stand behind what you sell.

Technology Tools for Customer Service

At a certain volume, you can't answer every message from scratch. You'll be typing the same shipping estimate, the same return policy explanation, the same "thanks for your order" dozens of times a week. Saved message templates inside eBay's platform handle the routine stuff so you can put real attention where it actually matters.

Write your templates to sound like a person, not a policy document. "Thanks for your order — your item ships tomorrow with tracking" is better than three paragraphs about processing times and delivery estimates. Buyers skim messages. Short and clear gets read; long and formal gets ignored.

Keep track of open conversations. Missing a buyer message is easy to do when you have fifty active listings and a day job, and eBay measures your response time. A missed message that sits unanswered for 24 hours hurts your metrics and occasionally turns a simple question into a case.

If you keep getting the same question about a particular listing — "does this fit a 2019 model?" "what are the exact dimensions?" — that's a signal to fix the listing, not just keep answering the question. Recurring inquiries are free feedback telling you where your description is falling short.

99

Good customer service on eBay isn't complicated. Respond quickly, describe things accurately, ship promptly, and handle problems without making buyers fight for resolutions they're entitled to. The sellers who do this consistently build reputations that generate repeat business and positive feedback with very little extra effort. The ones who treat service as an afterthought spend their time managing damage that compound into metric problems and account risk.

PART III: Advanced Selling Techniques

Chapter 12: eBay Stores and Subscription Benefits

I started with eBay's basic store subscription, paying $27.95 monthly for reduced listing fees and basic promotional tools. As my sales volume increased, I faced a decision about upgrading to higher-tier subscriptions that offered better fee structures and additional features.

The math seemed straightforward: higher monthly fees in exchange for lower per-transaction costs. But the reality proved more complex. Each subscription level included features I didn't need or use, and the fee savings only materialized at specific sales volumes that fluctuated monthly.

I spent several months tracking actual costs across different subscription levels, comparing total fees paid versus potential savings. The analysis revealed that subscription upgrades only made financial sense when sales exceeded consistent thresholds, and the additional features rarely generated enough extra revenue to justify their costs.

My current approach involves upgrading temporarily during peak selling seasons when volume justifies higher subscription costs, then downgrading during slower periods to minimize fixed expenses. This strategy requires monitoring and adjustment but maximizes profitability by aligning subscription costs with actual business needs.

eBay store subscriptions used to be genuinely optional — something serious sellers graduated into after building a real business. eBay has restructured that calculation. Fee discounts, search placement advantages, and marketing tools that non-subscribers can't access have made subscriptions less of an upgrade and more of a basic operating requirement for competitive selling.

The subscription model reflects eBay's shift toward professional sellers who treat the platform as a primary business channel rather than a casual selling outlet. Store subscriptions now function as the price of admission to competitive selling, not luxury upgrades for established businesses. Understanding when and how to use store benefits determines whether you can build a profitable eBay business or get priced out by better-equipped competitors.

Store Subscription Tier Analysis

eBay's store subscription structure creates artificial scarcity around features that should be standard for any serious selling platform. The basic store at $7.95 monthly provides modest improvements over free accounts, while higher tiers unlock progressively better benefits that can dramatically affect your profitability and competitive position.

> ◆ **Personal Experience:** When I restart selling on eBay after a long break, I always begin with the basic store subscription and scale up based on actual sales volume during the month. There's no point paying for premium features when you're testing the waters with limited inventory. Once I see consistent sales that justify higher fees, I'll upgrade to get better final value fee discounts and more free listings. It's much smarter to let your actual business performance drive subscription decisions rather than optimistically paying for features you might not use.

Basic store subscriptions offer 250 additional free listings monthly, bringing your total to 500 free listings compared to 250 for non-subscribers. The math works favorably if you regularly exceed the free listing threshold, but you need consistent inventory volume to justify the monthly fee through listing savings alone.

Premium store subscriptions at $27.95 monthly provide 1,000 free listings plus enhanced marketing tools and lower final value fees in some categories. The break-even point requires significant monthly sales volume, but active sellers often find the additional benefits justify the higher subscription cost through improved efficiency and reduced fees.

Anchor store subscriptions at $349.95 monthly target high-volume sellers with features like enhanced customer service tools, advanced marketing capabilities, and the lowest possible final value fees. These subscriptions only make sense for sellers generating substantial monthly revenue who can use the premium features effectively.

> ★ **Pro Tip:** Calculate your break-even point by tracking actual listing volumes and fee savings over three months before committing to higher-tier subscriptions.

Fee Structure Advantages

Store subscription fee benefits extend beyond simple listing cost reductions to include final value fee discounts that can significantly impact profitability for higher-volume sellers. The fee savings compound as your sales volume increases, making store subscriptions increasingly attractive as your business grows.

Final value fee reductions vary by category and subscription level, with anchor store subscribers receiving the best rates across all categories. These discounts can reduce your total transaction costs by 1-3%, which translates to meaningful profit improvements when applied across thousands of monthly transactions.

Fee caps provide protection against excessive charges on high-value items, with anchor and enterprise store subscribers enjoying lower maximum fees than basic sellers. These caps become important when selling expensive items where percentage-based fees would otherwise consume disproportionate portions of your profit margins.

The fee calculation changes frequently enough that yesterday's analysis might not reflect current economics. eBay adjusts fee structures regularly, often reducing some fees while increasing others in ways that affect different seller types differently.

Staying current with fee changes helps optimize your subscription level for maximum benefit.

Store Promotional Tools

eBay store promotional tools enable sophisticated marketing campaigns that increase sales through strategic discounting, customer retention, and inventory management. The Markdown Manager allows percentage or fixed-amount discounts across selected inventory, with crossed-out original prices that create urgency and perceived value for bargain hunters.

Email marketing tools build customer databases that enable direct communication about new inventory, sales events, and special offers that bypass eBay's search algorithm limitations. Promotional flyers that can be included with shipments encourage repeat purchases while providing professional touches that distinguish store sellers from casual operators. These tools work best when used strategically instead of constantly, preserving their impact while building genuine customer relationships.

★ **Pro Tip:** Use promotional tools strategically during slow periods or to move stale inventory. Constant sales devalue your regular pricing and train customers to wait for discounts.

Enhanced Search Visibility

eBay's algorithm provides preferential treatment to store subscribers through improved search placement and enhanced listing features that increase buyer exposure. These algorithmic advantages often provide more value than direct fee savings by driving higher sales volumes that justify subscription costs.

Better search placement produces more sales, which improves your metrics, which further improves search placement. This compounding effect is real and it's one of the actual arguments for store subscriptions beyond just the fee math — the algorithmic lift has value that's hard to quantify precisely but shows up in results.

Best Match search placement considers store subscription status as a ranking factor alongside price, shipping speed, and seller performance metrics. Store subscribers start with algorithmic advantages that help their listings achieve better visibility even when competing against identical items from non-subscribers.

Category-specific benefits vary across different product types, with some categories showing more pronounced advantages for store subscribers than others. Understanding how store benefits affect search placement in your specific categories helps determine whether subscription costs provide adequate returns on investment.

> ▲ **Caution:** Store subscription benefits diminish quickly if you don't maintain adequate inventory levels and listing activity to justify the monthly fees.

Marketing Tools and Promotional Features

Store subscriptions unlock marketing tools that individual sellers can't access through basic accounts. These promotional capabilities help drive traffic and sales in ways that often justify subscription costs through increased revenue rather than just fee savings.

Promoted listings discounts provide reduced advertising costs for store subscribers who want to boost listing visibility through paid placement. The advertising fee reductions can make promoted listings profitable for items where full-rate advertising costs wouldn't generate positive returns.

Email marketing capabilities allow store subscribers to build customer lists and send promotional messages to previous buyers. This direct marketing channel helps drive repeat sales and builds customer relationships that reduce dependence on eBay's search algorithm for traffic generation.

Cross-promotion tools help store subscribers showcase related items and encourage multiple purchases from individual buyers. These features increase average order values while providing better shopping experiences that encourage customer loyalty and repeat business.

Vacation settings and automated responses help professional sellers manage customer communications during absences without damaging seller metrics or losing sales opportunities. These tools become essential for sellers who want to maintain consistent operations while taking time away from their businesses.

Inventory Management Advantages

Store subscribers gain access to bulk listing tools and inventory management features that simplify operations for sellers managing large product catalogs. These efficiency improvements often provide more value than fee savings by reducing time investment required to maintain active listings.

Bulk editing capabilities allow store subscribers to modify pricing, shipping terms, and descriptions across multiple listings simultaneously. These tools become essential for sellers who need to adjust hundreds or thousands of listings in response to market conditions or supplier changes.

Good 'Til Cancelled listings provide automatic relisting for items that don't sell, eliminating manual relisting work that consumes time and creates gaps in inventory availability. This automation helps maintain consistent listing exposure while reducing administrative overhead.

Listing scheduling tools help store subscribers optimize listing timing for maximum visibility without requiring manual intervention. These features help maintain consistent listing activity and take advantage of peak shopping periods even when sellers aren't available to create listings manually.

> ■ **Danger Zone:** Don't upgrade to higher-tier store subscriptions based on projected growth. The economics only work when you have current sales volume that justifies the monthly fees.

Custom Store Design and Branding

Store customization options help subscribers create branded shopping experiences that differentiate their businesses from generic eBay listings. Professional store designs can improve buyer confidence and encourage repeat purchases by creating memorable shopping experiences.

> ◆ **Personal Experience:** I never bothered spending much time customizing my store design. It seemed like a lot of work for minimal return on investment. When someone wants to buy a rare Lego set, they care about authenticity, condition, and price - not whether my banner looks professional or my logo is perfectly branded. I'd rather spend that time sourcing better inventory or improving my listings than fiddling with store aesthetics that don't drive sales.

Analytics and Performance Tracking

Store subscriptions unlock eBay's traffic and sales analytics, which are worth using even if you're skeptical of dashboards. The data shows you which search terms are actually finding your listings, which items get clicks but don't sell (usually a pricing or photo problem), and which categories are producing real revenue versus just activity. Run these reports monthly and you'll spot problems before they compound into metric damage.

Return on Investment Calculation

Store subscription value depends heavily on your specific business model, sales volume, and operational needs. Sellers who primarily flip low-value items might never justify premium subscriptions, while sellers of higher-value items or large inventories often find the benefits pay for themselves quickly.

Monthly fee analysis should include not just direct fee savings but also time savings from automated features, increased sales from better search placement, and improved efficiency from enhanced tools. The total value proposition often exceeds simple fee calculations when you account for all benefits.

Break-even calculations need regular updates as your business evolves and eBay adjusts their fee structures and subscription benefits. What makes sense at one stage of business development might not remain optimal as your sales volume and operational complexity change.

Store subscription math needs revisiting whenever your sales volume changes significantly or eBay adjusts their fee structures. What made sense last year may not be optimal now. Track your actual costs and savings quarterly and adjust your subscription tier accordingly rather than assuming whatever you chose at the start is still the right fit.

eBay advertising used to be a few optional upgrades — bold titles, featured placement — that cost a few dollars and made a modest difference. The platform has since rebuilt its economics around paid visibility. Promoted listings now determine which items buyers actually see in crowded search results, and the sellers who don't participate get buried under the ones who do.

> ◆ **Personal Experience:** Early in my eBay career I avoided promoted listings entirely — the fees felt like unnecessary overhead when good listings should sell on their own. After months of watching certain items stall despite solid photos and competitive prices, I started experimenting. I priced items 15–20% higher than I would have otherwise, then used promoted listings to drive visibility, building the ad cost into the margin from the start. Items that had sat for weeks moved within days. I now promote almost everything. Faster inventory turnover at slightly lower margin usually beats slow sales at higher margin — and the promoted cost is just another line in the pricing math.

Understanding Promoted Listings Mechanics

Promoted listings function as eBay's primary advertising product, allowing sellers to pay for enhanced search placement in exchange for percentage-based fees calculated on final sale prices. The system promises better visibility and increased sales, but it operates through competitive bidding that can quickly escalate costs beyond profitable levels for inexperienced advertisers.

The bidding system requires sellers to set ad rates between 1% and 20% of item sale prices, with higher bids generally achieving better placement in search results and category pages. eBay's algorithm considers bid amounts alongside item relevance, seller performance, and buyer engagement metrics when determining which promoted listings receive premium placement.

> ◆ **Personal Experience:** I almost always set my listings to promoted these days. Without promotion, items take forever to sell in eBay's crowded marketplace. Sure, the advertising fee cuts into profit margins, but I just build that cost into my pricing from the start. An item that might sit for months without promotion will often sell within days when promoted, and faster inventory turnover usually beats slightly higher margins on items that move slowly.

Payment occurs only when promoted listings generate actual sales, not just clicks or impressions. This performance-based model reduces risk compared to traditional advertising, but it also means you pay advertising fees on top of regular eBay fees, further reducing profit margins on items that were already subject to substantial platform charges.

Promoted listings campaigns need active management. Bids that made sense in one competitive environment become wrong as other sellers adjust and seasonal patterns shift. Check your campaign performance monthly at minimum — not just to see if ads are running, but to verify the rates you're paying still make sense given your margins and what you're actually converting.

> ★ **Pro Tip:** Start with promoted listing campaigns at 3-5% ad rates and adjust based on actual performance data rather than eBay's suggested bid ranges, which tend to favor platform revenue over seller profitability.

Ad Rate Strategy and Optimization

Setting profitable ad rates requires understanding your profit margins, competition levels, and conversion rates in ways that many sellers never calculate accurately. Blindly following eBay's bid suggestions often results in advertising costs that exceed the incremental profit generated by promoted placements.

Profit margin analysis becomes crucial when determining maximum sustainable ad rates for different product categories and price points. Items with thin margins can't support high advertising rates, while products with substantial markup can justify more aggressive bidding for premium placement.

Competitive analysis reveals what other sellers are willing to pay for promoted placement in your categories. Understanding competitive bid levels helps you identify opportunities where lower bids might still achieve good placement, or categories where bidding wars make advertising unprofitable.

Performance tracking across different ad rates helps identify optimal bidding strategies for various types of inventory. Some items perform well with minimal promotion, while others require aggressive bidding to achieve visibility in crowded categories.

Category-specific strategies recognize that promoted listings work differently across various product types and buyer segments. Electronics buyers might respond well to promoted placement, while collectibles buyers often prefer to browse organically through detailed search filters.

Campaign Structure and Management

Promoted listings campaigns need actual management, not just setup. Sellers who create a campaign and walk away often discover months later that their ad rates are either too high to be profitable or too low to achieve the placement they expected. The market shifts. Competitors change their bids. What worked in January looks different in July.

Campaign segmentation helps isolate performance data for different product types, price ranges, and seasonal categories. Running separate campaigns for different inventory segments provides clearer performance insights and enables more targeted optimization strategies.

Budget management prevents advertising costs from spiraling beyond profitable levels during competitive periods or seasonal demand spikes. Setting maximum monthly advertising budgets helps control total promotional spending while allowing flexibility for high-performing campaigns.

Seasonal adjustment strategies recognize that optimal ad rates change throughout the year as competition intensity and buyer behavior patterns shift. Holiday seasons often require higher bids to maintain visibility, while off-peak periods might allow profitable promotion at lower rates.

Performance monitoring requires tracking not just promoted listing metrics but also overall account performance to understand how advertising affects organic search placement and total sales velocity.

> ▲ **Caution:** Promoted listings can become addictive when sellers see increased sales without calculating whether the advertising costs justify the revenue improvements.

ROI Calculation and Profitability Analysis

More sales isn't the same as more profit. This distinction kills more promoted listings strategies than anything else. Calculate your true ROI by accounting for all costs — eBay fees, promoted listing fees, shipping, item cost, time — not just the sale price minus the ad rate. An item that nets $2 after all costs but costs $1.50 in promotion is not a success story.

True ROI calculations must account for eBay fees, shipping costs, item costs, and time investment in addition to promoted listings fees. The total cost structure often reveals that apparently successful campaigns actually reduce overall profitability despite generating higher sales volume.

Incremental sales analysis helps distinguish between sales that resulted from promoted placement versus organic sales that would have occurred anyway. This distinction determines whether advertising costs generate genuine incremental revenue or just expensive visibility for sales that were already likely to happen.

Break-even analysis reveals the minimum performance levels required for promoted listings campaigns to generate positive returns. Understanding these thresholds helps identify which products and categories can support profitable advertising investment.

Long-term impact assessment considers how promoted listings affect organic search performance and overall seller metrics that influence future visibility. Some sellers find that aggressive promotion improves their overall search ranking, while others see diminishing organic performance when they reduce advertising spending.

Bidding Psychology and Competitive Dynamics

eBay's promoted listings auction creates psychological pressure that encourages overbidding as sellers compete for premium placement without carefully calculating profitability implications. Understanding these psychological traps helps maintain disciplined bidding strategies that protect profit margins.

Bid escalation often occurs when sellers react emotionally to losing visibility rather than analytically evaluating whether higher bids generate profitable returns. The auction format encourages competitive responses that can quickly drive advertising costs beyond sustainable levels.

Market timing affects optimal bidding strategies as competition intensity varies throughout days, weeks, and seasons. Understanding these patterns helps optimize ad spending by bidding more aggressively during high-conversion periods and reducing bids when competition is fierce but conversion rates are poor.

Competitor analysis reveals bidding patterns and strategies that successful sellers use in your categories. Monitoring competitive behavior helps identify opportunities for efficient bidding and categories where advertising competition makes promotion unprofitable.

> ■ **Danger Zone:** Never increase promoted listings bids without calculating the specific profit impact. Many sellers chase visibility without understanding whether increased placement generates profitable sales.

Alternative Advertising Options

eBay offers advanced promoted listings campaigns and offsite advertising programs beyond the standard bidding system. Advanced campaigns extend placement to eBay's partner sites. Offsite programs charge only on sales generated from external traffic. Both require larger budgets and more active management than standard promoted listings, and the returns are harder to measure because the attribution is murkier. Most sellers are better served by getting standard promoted listings working well first before exploring either of these options.

Performance Monitoring and Analytics

eBay's advertising analytics show you click-through rates, impressions, and sales attributed to promoted listings. Use them. These numbers tell you which items are attracting attention but not converting (likely a pricing or listing quality problem), which items convert well (candidates for higher promotion), and which items generate no interest even when promoted (usually not an ad problem — usually a listing or market problem).

Click-through rate analysis reveals which promoted listings generate buyer interest and which fail to attract attention despite premium placement. Low click-through rates often indicate pricing problems, poor listing quality, or inappropriate targeting that advertising can't overcome.

Conversion rate tracking shows which promoted listings turn browser interest into actual sales. High click-through rates with poor conversion often indicate listing optimization problems that waste advertising spending on unqualified traffic.

Cost per acquisition metrics help evaluate whether promoted listings generate customers at sustainable costs compared to other marketing channels and organic acquisition methods. Understanding true customer acquisition costs helps optimize promotional spending across different strategies.

Attribution analysis attempts to understand how promoted listings interact with organic search performance and repeat customer behavior. These complex relationships affect the true value of advertising investment beyond immediate campaign metrics.

Seasonal and Market Timing

Promoted listings effectiveness varies dramatically based on seasonal demand patterns, competitive intensity, and market conditions that affect both bidding costs and conversion rates. Professional sellers adjust their advertising strategies to match these changing conditions.

Holiday season advertising often requires higher bids to maintain visibility as competition intensifies, but the increased conversion rates and average order values can justify higher promotional spending during peak shopping periods.

Off-season promotion strategies focus on maintaining visibility during slow periods when organic traffic declines but competition for promoted placement also decreases. Lower bidding costs during off-peak periods can provide cost-effective traffic generation.

Product lifecycle considerations recognize that optimal promoted listings strategies change as items move from new releases through mainstream popularity to clearance phases. Each lifecycle stage requires different bidding approaches and performance expectations.

When a category becomes saturated with promoted listings, the cost to achieve meaningful placement goes up and the incremental value of each position goes down. Watch your cost-per-sale in categories where you promote. When it starts climbing without a corresponding improvement in conversion, the category may be over-advertised — a signal to reduce bids rather than raise them.

Promoted listings are a tool, not a strategy. Used well — with known margins, tracked performance, and rates that still leave you profitable — they solve a real problem. Used badly — bid up reactively, applied indiscriminately, never measured against actual profit — they eat your margins while creating the illusion of success. Run the real numbers before you run the campaigns.

International selling is genuinely worth considering if you have the right inventory — and genuinely not worth considering if you don't. The Global Shipping Program removed most of the technical barriers, but the business case still depends on whether international buyers want what you have at prices that justify the additional paperwork and longer dispute timelines. The opportunity is real. So is the complexity.

Market Research for Global Opportunities

Before building international selling systems, check whether there's actually demand for your specific inventory at prices that make the extra complexity worthwhile. Many sellers discover that international buyers exist for their product category but won't pay enough above domestic prices to justify the additional customs paperwork, longer shipping times, and harder-to-resolve disputes. Research completed international sales in your categories first.

Currency strength and exchange rate trends affect international buyer behavior in ways that impact your pricing strategy and market selection. Buyers from countries with strong currencies relative to the dollar often accept higher prices, while buyers from countries with weak currencies become extremely price-sensitive and focus on finding bargains.

Regional demand patterns often differ dramatically from domestic markets, creating opportunities for products that perform poorly in the US but generate strong international interest. Vintage American products, regional food specialties, and items with cultural significance often command premium prices in international markets where they're rare or unavailable locally.

Competitive analysis in international markets reveals whether you're entering crowded spaces or finding underserved niches. Some product categories face intense competition from local sellers in major international markets, while others offer opportunities for US sellers who can provide unique products or superior service.

★ **Pro Tip:** Research completed international sales in your categories to understand actual demand and pricing patterns before committing to global expansion strategies.

Cultural Considerations and Communication

International buyers often have different expectations about communication style, response timing, and business practices that affect their willingness to purchase from US sellers. Understanding these cultural differences helps build trust and confidence that leads to successful transactions and positive feedback.

The practical version: respond within 24 hours regardless of time zone, write in plain direct English without idioms or slang, and don't assume that a terse message means a hostile buyer. Many international buyers write briefly because English is their second language, not because they're difficult. Treat directness as efficiency, not rudeness, and you'll have far fewer miscommunications.

Advanced Shipping and Logistics

Direct international shipping provides more control and potentially better profit margins than eBay's Global Shipping Program, but it requires understanding customs requirements, prohibited items, and shipping carrier limitations that vary across different destination countries.

Shipping carrier selection affects both costs and delivery reliability for international packages. Different carriers excel in different regions, and understanding these strengths helps optimize shipping choices for various international destinations.

Customs forms need accurate values and honest content descriptions. Buyers sometimes ask you to under-declare to reduce their import duties — don't do it. Packages held by customs, unexpected duty charges landing on your buyer, and customs fraud penalties are all worse outcomes than whatever goodwill you'd earn by cooperating with the request.

Insurance and tracking options vary significantly for international shipments, affecting both your protection against loss and buyer confidence in their purchase. Understanding these options helps balance cost control with risk management for valuable international shipments.

▲ **Caution:** Never ship internationally without comprehensive tracking and insurance coverage. International shipping disputes are much more difficult to resolve than domestic issues.

Tax and Legal Compliance

International selling creates tax obligations and legal responsibilities that many sellers discover only after problems arise. Understanding these requirements upfront prevents costly mistakes and compliance issues that can damage your business.

Sales tax collection requirements continue evolving as governments expand their reach into international e-commerce transactions. Some international sales may require collecting and remitting taxes to foreign governments, creating administrative burdens that affect profitability calculations.

Import/export regulations restrict certain products from crossing international borders, and violations can result in confiscated packages, fines, and legal problems. Understanding these restrictions helps avoid shipping items that create compliance issues.

Business license requirements may apply to sellers who develop substantial international sales volumes. Some jurisdictions require export licenses or business registrations for sellers who exceed certain international sales thresholds.

Product liability considerations become more complex when selling internationally because different countries have varying consumer protection laws and legal systems. Understanding these differences helps assess risks and adjust business practices appropriately.

Currency and Financial Management

Exchange rate fluctuations affect international pricing strategies and profit margins in ways that require ongoing attention and sometimes hedging strategies to manage currency risk effectively.

Payment processing for international transactions involves additional fees and processing times that affect cash flow and profitability calculations. Understanding these costs helps price items appropriately while maintaining competitive positioning.

Currency conversion timing can significantly impact profit margins when exchange rates fluctuate between sale and payment processing. Some sellers develop strategies for managing this timing risk through pricing adjustments or financial instruments.

International payment disputes follow different procedures and timelines than domestic issues, often requiring more documentation and patience to resolve satisfactorily.

> ■ **Danger Zone:** Never assume international transactions will process as smoothly as domestic sales. Plan for longer processing times, additional fees, and more complex dispute resolution procedures.

Building International Customer Relationships

Successful international selling often depends on developing repeat customers who appreciate your products and service quality enough to justify the additional costs and complexities of cross-border transactions.

For international sales, problems that escalate are harder to resolve and more damaging when they result in negative feedback. A buyer in Germany or Japan has fewer options than a domestic buyer if something goes wrong, which makes them more likely to leave feedback than open a case. Get ahead of problems fast. Communicate clearly. Resolve issues even when the cost feels disproportionate — international feedback damage tends to be.

International buyers often communicate more formally or more briefly than US buyers, and messages that read as curt in English are often just normal in their language. Don't interpret directness as hostility. Write your responses clearly, skip the idioms, and don't assume shared context that only applies domestically.

International buyers who've had good experiences are worth following up with — a brief message after delivery confirming everything arrived well costs nothing and often produces positive feedback that took effort to earn. International repeat customers are valuable because acquiring them the first time involved more friction than domestic buyers. Worth keeping.

International buyers leave feedback at different rates and in different patterns than domestic buyers. Some markets have cultures of more effusive positive feedback; others rarely leave it at all even after successful transactions. Don't read a lack of feedback from international buyers as dissatisfaction — follow up gently if you want a response, but don't chase it.

Seasonal and Regional Market Timing

International markets operate on different seasonal cycles and holiday patterns that create opportunities for counter-seasonal selling when domestic demand is low.

International holiday calendars differ significantly from US ones. Christmas ships later to some markets, Diwali and Lunar New Year drive purchasing spikes that US sellers often miss, and shipping lead times to most international destinations add weeks to delivery windows. Build those lead times into your holiday planning or you'll be shipping things that arrive after the occasion they were bought for.

Shipping lead time planning becomes more complex for international sales because longer transit times require earlier order placement to make sure holiday delivery, affecting inventory planning and promotional timing.

Regional economic conditions and events can dramatically affect international buyer behavior and purchasing power in ways that require monitoring and adaptation of international selling strategies.

Technology Tools for Global Selling

International selling software helps manage the additional complexity of cross-border transactions through automation tools that handle currency conversion, tax calculation, and shipping documentation.

Translation tools assist with communication and listing optimization for international markets, though they require careful review to make sure accuracy and cultural appropriateness.

Market research platforms provide data about international demand, pricing, and competition that helps identify opportunities and optimize strategies for different global markets.

Analytics tools help track international performance separately from domestic sales, enabling optimization of global strategies based on actual performance data rather than assumptions about international buyer behavior.

International selling is worth pursuing if you have the patience to learn the additional requirements and the right inventory for it. Certain categories — vintage American products, items with US cultural cachet, specialized goods that aren't readily available elsewhere — can generate strong international demand with good margins. Others are a waste of the effort. Know which bucket you're in before you commit to building global systems.

Chapter 15: Seasonal Selling and Market Timing

Seasonal selling sounds simple — list Christmas items in November, swimwear in spring, Halloween costumes in October. Those patterns still hold. What's changed is the competition around them. You're not just up against other individual sellers anymore. You're competing against retailers who bought six months ago, automated repricing systems that react in real time, and overseas suppliers who flood every mainstream seasonal category at exactly the moment demand peaks. Timing and sourcing discipline matter more than they used to.

Understanding Modern Seasonal Cycles

Traditional seasonal patterns have compressed and shifted as retailers extend holiday shopping seasons and buyers develop year-round purchasing habits driven by online convenience and global shipping availability. Christmas shopping now begins in October, back-to-school buying starts in June, and Halloween merchandise appears in August alongside early Christmas items.

Early bird shoppers create opportunities for sellers who can anticipate seasonal demand and list inventory before mainstream retailers flood markets with competing products. These buyers often pay premium prices for early access to seasonal items and represent higher-value customers who plan purchases in advance.

Extended shopping seasons mean seasonal items maintain value for longer periods, but they also face more sustained competition as the selling window stretches across multiple months. Understanding when demand peaks and when competition becomes overwhelming helps optimize listing timing and pricing strategies.

Counter-seasonal opportunities emerge when domestic seasonal patterns don't align with international markets or when sellers can find buyers preparing for opposite-hemisphere seasons. Australian buyers need winter coats in July, creating opportunities for US sellers to move cold-weather inventory during summer months.

Inventory Planning and Sourcing Timing

Successful seasonal selling requires purchasing inventory months before selling seasons begin, which means tying up capital in products that won't generate revenue for extended periods while accurately predicting demand for items that might not perform as expected.

Wholesale buying cycles for seasonal merchandise often close six months before retail seasons, forcing sellers to commit to inventory purchases based on predictions about buyer demand and competitive conditions that won't be validated until much later.

Storage capacity planning becomes crucial when seasonal inventory temporarily doubles or triples space requirements during build-up periods. Many sellers underestimate the physical space needed for holiday inventory and find themselves cramped for workspace during their busiest selling periods.

Clearance timing strategy determines whether seasonal inventory becomes profitable merchandise or expensive mistakes. Items that don't sell during peak seasons often become nearly worthless, requiring aggressive clearance pricing that can result in substantial losses on unsold inventory.

Risk management through diversified seasonal portfolios helps reduce the impact of individual seasonal categories that underperform expectations. Spreading seasonal investments across multiple holidays and categories provides protection against total losses when specific seasonal bets fail.

Holiday Season Optimization

Holiday selling represents the make-or-break period for many seasonal sellers, when months of preparation and inventory investment either generate substantial profits or create expensive lessons in market timing and buyer psychology.

Pre-holiday positioning requires listing seasonal inventory early enough to capture early shoppers while avoiding getting lost in the flood of competing merchandise that appears as seasons approach peak demand periods.

Gift-focused marketing becomes crucial during holiday periods when buyers purchase items for others rather than themselves. Understanding gift-giving psychology and presentation requirements helps optimize listings for buyers who prioritize presentation and gift-appropriateness over personal utility.

> ▲ **Caution:** Never promise holiday delivery dates you can't guarantee. Disappointed holiday buyers leave the most damaging negative feedback and create customer service nightmares.

Shipping deadline management creates operational challenges when holiday buyers expect guaranteed delivery dates that require precise coordination of inventory availability, order processing speed, and carrier performance during peak shipping periods.

Last-minute buyer behavior creates opportunities for sellers who maintain inventory and fast shipping capabilities when other sellers run out of stock or can't meet delivery deadlines. These desperate buyers often pay premium prices for items they need urgently.

Clearance and Transition Strategies

Post-season clearance requires balancing the need to recover inventory investment against the reality that seasonal items lose most of their value when seasons end. Successful clearance strategies help minimize losses while freeing up capital and storage space for next season's inventory.

Gradual markdown strategies often generate better total returns than dramatic clearance pricing because they maintain perceived value while testing price sensitivity among remaining buyers. Steep initial discounts can signal desperation and reduce overall clearance revenue.

International market opportunities can extend seasonal selling periods by targeting buyers in different geographic regions where seasons or cultural celebrations occur at different times. Winter items in the Northern Hemisphere can find buyers in southern hemisphere markets during their winter seasons.

Transition timing to next season's inventory requires careful coordination between clearance activities and new inventory acquisition. Moving too quickly can result in lost clearance revenue, while moving too slowly can miss optimal purchasing opportunities for next season's merchandise.

Storage decisions for unsold seasonal inventory involve choosing between holding items for next year's season versus liquidating immediately to free up capital for other opportunities. These decisions depend on storage costs, capital requirements, and confidence in future demand predictions.

Non-Traditional Seasonal Opportunities

Beyond the obvious holidays, smaller seasonal windows are worth knowing: back-to-school in August, graduation season in May and June, sports equipment around league start dates, tax season office supplies in February and March, and cultural and religious observances that mainstream retailers consistently underserve. None of these are as large as Christmas, but they're also less crowded — and a seller who sources early and lists before demand peaks gets the premium pricing window that latecomers don't.

Market Timing Beyond Seasonality

Effective market timing extends beyond seasonal patterns to include economic cycles, news events, and cultural trends that create temporary demand spikes for specific types of merchandise.

Economic uncertainty often increases demand for preparedness supplies, investment-related items, and practical goods while reducing demand for luxury and discretionary purchases. Understanding these economic cycles helps adjust inventory strategies for changing buyer priorities.

News-driven demand can create sudden opportunities for items related to current events, but these opportunities often disappear as quickly as they appear, requiring fast response times and flexible inventory management.

Viral trends and social media influences create unpredictable demand spikes for specific products that can generate substantial profits for sellers who can respond quickly, but these trends can also disappear without warning, leaving sellers with worthless inventory.

Product lifecycle timing affects optimal selling periods for electronics, collectibles, and other items whose value changes predictably based on product release cycles, discontinuation announcements, and technology obsolescence patterns.

Competitive Intelligence and Market Monitoring

Watch what competitors are doing with seasonal inventory — when they're building stock, when they're running clearance, when they're dropping prices. Seller forums, completed sales data, and basic observation of active listings in your categories tell you a lot about what other sellers know about the market. Getting ahead of patterns that are already obvious to experienced sellers in your category is the job.

Seasonal selling works best when you treat it as a system rather than a reaction. Know your categories, know your lead times, buy before demand peaks and sell before it drops, and have a clearance plan for what doesn't move. The sellers who get hurt by seasonality are the ones who buy speculatively without accounting for the risk that their timing is off.

PART IV: Dropshipping on eBay

Chapter 16: Dropshipping Basics and Setup

Dropshipping on eBay used to be a gray area where you could find wholesale suppliers, list their products without holding inventory, and build a real income with minimal upfront investment. That window is mostly closed now. Not because eBay changed its policies, though it did, but because platforms like Temu and DHgate turned the entire model inside out. Sellers can now list hundreds of thousands of identical items directly from overseas warehouses with one-click automation. The playing field isn't just tilted anymore. For most generic product categories, it's gone.

This chapter covers how dropshipping works on eBay today, what the rules are, and what's required to run it properly. But read it with clear eyes: the easy money version of this model is dead. What remains is possible but genuinely difficult, and it requires finding niches where automation hasn't already wiped out the margins.

eBay's Dropshipping Policy Evolution

eBay tightened its dropshipping policies as the overseas flooding got worse, and the requirements it now enforces would have seemed unreasonable to dropshippers five years ago. The platform requires you to meet the same delivery standards as inventory-based sellers, manage all returns yourself, and be the identified seller on every communication and package — even when your supplier is the one actually shipping the goods.

Your name is on the listing. Your account takes the hit if something goes wrong. If your supplier ships late, ships wrong, or ships garbage, eBay holds you responsible — not them. You can't point buyers at your supplier or disclaim responsibility for what shows up at their door. That's the deal, and it's non-negotiable.

Delivery speed is where most overseas dropshipping operations fail eBay's standards. A buyer in Ohio does not want to wait three weeks for something shipped from Shenzhen. eBay's algorithm buries sellers with slow delivery metrics and its enforcement has gotten less forgiving, not more. If your supplier can't meet reasonable US shipping windows, the business model doesn't work on this platform.

Returns are your problem, full stop. When a buyer opens a return case and your supplier is unresponsive, you're eating the cost. Build that into your margin calculations from day one, because it will happen and it will be more frequent than you expect.

eBay also prohibits listing items you don't have a confirmed supplier relationship for. You cannot find a product on Temu, list it on eBay, and then scramble to order it after it sells. You need established supplier access and confirmed availability before the listing goes live.

> ★ **Pro Tip:** Read eBay's current dropshipping policies thoroughly before starting any dropshipping operation. These policies change frequently and violations can result in immediate account suspension.

Legitimate Supplier Identification and Vetting

Finding a supplier who is actually worth working with is harder than the YouTube dropshipping courses make it sound. The legitimate wholesale market has been so thoroughly gamed by overseas operators that distinguishing a real supplier from a middleman pretending to be one requires real due diligence. Fake supplier directories are a business unto themselves — they charge monthly fees and deliver lists of scammers.

Real wholesalers require actual business credentials — a reseller certificate, a tax ID, sometimes a minimum order commitment. A supplier who will sell to anyone with a credit card, no questions asked, is almost certainly not a legitimate wholesaler. That ease of access is a red flag, not a convenience.

Order samples before you commit to any supplier relationship. What a product looks like in catalog photos and what arrives in a buyer's mailbox are often two different things. If you won't personally buy and inspect a product before listing it, you have no business listing it. The reviews that destroy accounts usually come from sellers who trusted supplier photos.

Even good suppliers have bad months. Track shipping times, order accuracy, and communication responsiveness on an ongoing basis. A supplier who was reliable for six months can deteriorate without warning — factory problems, staffing changes, fulfillment partner switches. By the time the negative feedback starts rolling in, the damage is already done.

Always have a backup. Single-supplier dropshipping businesses are one stockout or one relationship breakdown away from zero inventory and active listings pointing at nothing. The redundancy feels unnecessary until the day it isn't.

Financial Structure and Pricing Models

The margins in dropshipping look better on paper than they are in practice. Take your supplier cost, add eBay's final value fee (typically 12–15%), add payment processing, add return shipping for the percentage of orders that come back, add your time for customer service, and add the cost of the occasional supplier mistake you absorb without reimbursement. What looked like a $12 profit on a $40 item often ends up closer to $4 after everything.

Cash flow timing is a real problem that catches new dropshippers off guard. You pay your supplier when the order comes in. eBay holds your payout on a schedule that may not align with that. In a busy week you can be float-financing dozens of orders before a dollar hits your bank account. Have working capital before you start, not after you run out.

Do the full margin math before listing anything. Not the optimistic version — the realistic one that accounts for fees, returns, and things going wrong. If the numbers only work when everything goes perfectly, the model doesn't work.

Competing on price against sellers who source directly from the same Chinese factories you're dropshipping from is a losing game. They have no middleman markup. You do. The only way to justify a higher price is to offer something they don't — faster shipping, better descriptions, more reliable service, or a niche where they haven't bothered to compete yet.

International suppliers add currency conversion costs and payment processing fees that eat further into margins. Build these into your calculations rather than discovering them later. A supplier quoted in yuan that seemed profitable can look different after conversion and transaction fees are applied.

▲ **Caution:** Never start dropshipping without sufficient working capital to cover at least 30 days of supplier payments while waiting for eBay payment processing and potential return situations.

Operational Systems and Workflow Management

Dropshipping has more moving parts than inventory-based selling, and each handoff between you and your supplier is a place where things can break. The operational systems aren't optional — they're what keep a mistake with one order from becoming a mistake with fifty.

Every order needs to get to your supplier with the correct buyer address, item specifications, and any special instructions. An error here means a wrong item shipped to a wrong address — which you'll discover two weeks later when a buyer opens a case. Automate the order forwarding and confirm it's working before you scale up listings.

Supplier stock levels can change without warning. An item that was available yesterday is out of stock today, and if your listing is still live, someone might buy it before you know. Real-time inventory synchronization between your supplier and your eBay listings is not a nice-to-have — it's the difference between running a business and constantly putting out fires.

Your quality standards are only as good as your supplier's willingness to maintain them. Periodic spot checks — ordering items yourself and inspecting what arrives — are the only reliable way to know what buyers are actually receiving. Discovering a quality problem through buyer complaints is the expensive way to find out.

Buyer inquiries move fast on eBay. When a question comes in about an order status or delivery timeline and your supplier is the one with that information, you're in the middle trying to pass messages back and forth. Build communication workflows that let you answer buyers quickly even when you're dependent on a third party for the facts.

Get tracking numbers uploaded to eBay the moment your supplier generates them, not when you get around to it. Late tracking uploads hurt your metrics and create buyer anxiety that turns into messages you'll spend time answering.

> ■ **Danger Zone:** Never dropship without systems that provide real-time visibility into supplier inventory levels and order status. Blind dropshipping operations inevitably create customer service disasters.

Legal and Compliance Considerations

Most dropshippers don't think about legal liability until something goes wrong. The practical reality is simple: if you sell it, you're responsible for it. Your supplier being overseas and unreachable doesn't change that. If a product you dropshipped causes harm — a faulty electrical item, a toy with unsafe parts — the claim comes to you, not the factory in Guangdong.

Avoid categories with meaningful safety risk — electronics, children's items, health products — unless you've verified the supplier's certifications and have documentation to back them up. The margins on cheap consumer electronics rarely justify the exposure.

Check whether your state or local jurisdiction requires any business registration or reseller permit for dropshipping. Requirements vary widely and ignoring them doesn't make them not apply to you.

eBay collects sales tax automatically in most US states, which removes one headache. Income tax is still your responsibility. Dropshipping income is business income, and the IRS treats it that way regardless of how casual your operation feels.

International shipping from suppliers to US buyers can trigger customs issues that your buyer, and therefore you, have to deal with. Know what your supplier is shipping, what country it's coming from, and whether anything in your catalog is subject to import restrictions or duties that could create problems at the border.

Technology Integration and Automation

The software side of dropshipping is where the business either runs or collapses. Without automation connecting your eBay listings to your supplier's inventory, you're manually checking stock levels and updating prices — which means you'll always be behind, and overselling is inevitable.

Tools like DSM Tool, AutoDS, and similar platforms integrate with eBay and major suppliers to handle listing creation, price updates, order forwarding, and tracking uploads. They're not free, and they're not magic — but running a dropshipping operation without one of them is like trying to manage a warehouse inventory on paper.

Test your order automation before you have real buyers depending on it. Place test orders, verify that supplier information transmits correctly, confirm that tracking flows back to eBay. The failure mode you want to find is the one that happens in testing, not the one you discover because a buyer opened a case.

Keep close watch on which products are actually profitable after all costs. The temptation with dropshipping software is to list thousands of items and let volume compensate for thin margins. That strategy works until a category gets flooded, a supplier raises prices, or a cluster of returns wipes out a month of gains in a week.

Watch your supplier performance metrics the same way you watch your seller metrics. Delivery time trends, order accuracy rates, response times when problems arise — these numbers tell you whether a supplier relationship is working before buyers start telling you it isn't.

Performance Monitoring and Optimization

Monitor supplier delivery performance weekly, not monthly. Problems compound fast in dropshipping. A supplier whose on-time rate drops from 95% to 80% over a month will show up in your feedback and your eBay metrics before you notice the pattern in a monthly review.

Cut products that cause disproportionate problems. Some items generate returns, disputes, and negative feedback at a rate that makes the sales not worth having. A product with a 15% return rate isn't a pricing problem — it's a product problem. Stop listing it.

Periodically search eBay for your own listings, or products identical to yours, to see what you're actually competing against. If the same item is now listed by fifty sellers at prices below your cost, that category is done for you. Move on before it drags your metrics down.

The honest summary of eBay dropshipping in 2025 is this: the broad generic product model is broken. Temu, DHgate, and AliExpress-connected sellers have flooded every mainstream category with automated listings at prices that leave no room for a middleman. What still works — and it does still work, is finding niches that automation hasn't saturated yet. Specialty parts, regional items, products that require actual product knowledge to source and describe accurately. The window gets narrower every year, but it isn't closed.

If you're going to try it, go in with realistic expectations, real supplier relationships, proper systems, and a specific niche in mind. Anyone telling you eBay dropshipping is a path to passive income with minimal effort is selling you something that stopped being true years ago.

Finding a good supplier is genuinely hard work, and the difficulty has increased as the fake supplier industry has matured. There are now entire businesses built around selling access to supplier lists that lead nowhere, charging monthly fees for catalogs full of middlemen marking up the same AliExpress products you could find yourself in twenty minutes. Separating legitimate wholesale sources from these operations requires a process, not just optimism.

Distinguishing Legitimate Wholesalers from Scammers

The simplest test: a real wholesale supplier doesn't need to recruit you. They have buyers. They're not running ads promising passive income or charging a monthly fee to access their catalog. When you reach out to a legitimate wholesaler, they want to know if you're a real business — not sell you on the opportunity. If the pitch is going the other direction, walk away.

The red flags are consistent: upfront fees to "access wholesale pricing," catalogs full of generic product photos clearly pulled from other sites, vague answers about shipping times, and high-pressure urgency about getting started before the opportunity disappears. Legitimate suppliers are boring to sign up with. That's a feature, not a bug.

Verify before you commit. Search the supplier's business name against state registration databases. Look for a real physical address, not a PO box, and confirm it exists. Call the phone number. These steps take thirty minutes and eliminate ninety percent of scam operations, which generally can't survive basic verification.

Real wholesalers give you clear pricing, clear terms, and clear shipping costs up front. They don't bury fees or require you to pay for information about how their business works. Opacity in the pricing structure is almost always covering something you wouldn't agree to if you saw it clearly.

Ask for references from other resellers and actually contact them. Most scam operations either refuse or provide references who are part of the same network. A supplier who gives you the names of three resellers who will independently confirm their experience is giving you something worth having.

> ★ **Pro Tip:** Never work with suppliers who require upfront fees, refuse to provide business credentials, or pressure you to make immediate decisions without proper due diligence time.

Domestic vs. International Supplier Trade-offs

Domestic suppliers cost more per unit and offer less selection. That's the trade-off, and it's real. But for eBay dropshipping specifically, the shipping speed advantage of a US-based supplier is worth more than most sellers realize. eBay's algorithm rewards fast shipping, buyers expect Amazon-style timelines, and a supplier who ships in two days from a US warehouse competes completely differently than one shipping from overseas.

International suppliers — primarily Chinese operations — offer lower unit costs but come with real problems that eat into those savings. The Temu and DHgate model has demonstrated exactly what happens when overseas operations run unchecked: identical products listed by thousands of sellers, three-week shipping windows, and a race to the bottom on price that nobody wins.

The shipping speed math is blunt: domestic suppliers typically deliver in one to three business days. International suppliers typically take two to four weeks. On eBay in 2025, that difference is not a minor inconvenience — it's the difference between competitive and invisible.

Quality consistency is harder to maintain with international suppliers. Standards vary more widely, packaging is often substandard, and when something goes wrong the time zone gap and language barrier make resolution slow. What takes a quick phone call with a US supplier can take days of back-and-forth with an overseas one.

If you work with international suppliers, factor in the full cost picture: longer customer service cycles, higher return rates, currency conversion fees, and the real possibility that a buyer opens a case before their package even clears customs. The margin that looked attractive on a spreadsheet can disappear entirely once those costs are counted.

The honest recommendation for most eBay dropshippers is to prioritize domestic suppliers even at higher unit costs. The speed advantage, the simpler compliance picture, and the reduced customer service burden usually make up the cost difference — and often more than make up for it.

Supplier Evaluation and Due Diligence

Evaluate every potential supplier the same way, regardless of how good they seem on paper. The process is straightforward and takes a few days: order samples, time the delivery, inspect what arrives, send a test inquiry to their support and see how they respond. This tells you more than any catalog, website, or sales conversation.

Order samples of the specific items you plan to list — not their showroom items, not whatever they recommend. The product you're going to sell to real buyers. Examine the packaging, the condition, and how closely it matches the photos. If there's a gap between what you see in the catalog and what shows up at your door, there will be the same gap for your buyers.

Note the actual delivery time, not the promised one. Many suppliers quote shipping windows that reflect best-case scenarios rather than typical performance. Test it multiple times at different points in the week and month. A supplier who ships fast when they're trying to win your business may slow down considerably once you're a regular account.

Submit a problem to their customer service before you depend on them for real orders. Report a fake issue with a sample order and see how they handle it. Response speed, quality of communication, and willingness to resolve it tells you exactly what your buyers will experience when something goes wrong — and something will go wrong.

Get their return policy in writing and read it carefully. A supplier whose return policy requires items to be returned to China at buyer expense on a $15 product effectively has no return policy. That becomes your problem when you have to absorb the cost to keep your eBay standing intact.

Look for signs of financial instability: social media with no activity, a website that hasn't been updated in years, non-responses to email during business hours. Suppliers that go dark mid-relationship leave you with active listings pointing at inventory you can't fulfill.

> ▲ **Caution:** Always test suppliers with small orders before committing to large-scale business relationships. Many suppliers perform well initially but fail when order volumes increase.

Building Professional Supplier Relationships

The best supplier relationships develop the same way any good business relationship does: through reliability, communication, and mutual benefit over time. Suppliers who have been around long enough have seen the full range of buyers — from serious resellers who pay on time and communicate clearly to one-time buyers who disappear after the first problem. They know the difference quickly.

Communicate like a professional. Answer their messages promptly. When you have a problem, describe it clearly rather than just expressing frustration. Suppliers who trust you respond faster, help you solve problems more readily, and occasionally give you advance notice about stock changes or pricing shifts that other accounts find out about after the fact.

Pay on time, every time. It sounds obvious, but it's the single fastest way to move from "new account" to "preferred customer." Suppliers who have consistent, reliable payers give them priority when stock is limited and are more likely to work with you when something goes sideways.

Order consistently rather than in erratic bursts. A supplier who gets steady orders from you every week plans around you. A supplier who gets huge orders occasionally followed by silence doesn't invest in the relationship because they're not sure if you'll be back.

Tell them what's selling and what isn't. Suppliers who understand your market can help you source better. If a particular product keeps coming back because it doesn't match the listing photos, saying so gives them useful feedback and positions you as a serious partner rather than just another account number.

As your volume grows, ask for better terms. Most suppliers have pricing tiers they don't advertise. The ask is usually as simple as "I've been ordering consistently for six months — is there anything you can do on pricing at this volume?" The worst answer is no.

Contract Terms and Agreement Negotiation

Read every agreement before you sign it. That sounds obvious, but sellers in a hurry to get started skip this and discover the problems later. Pay particular attention to minimum order commitments, exclusivity clauses, and what happens to your pricing if those commitments aren't met.

Minimum order requirements are a common sticking point for new dropshippers. If a supplier requires a $500 monthly minimum to maintain wholesale pricing, you need to know that before you build listings around their products. Missing the minimum mid-relationship usually means a price increase that breaks your margin calculations.

Be cautious with exclusivity. A supplier offering you exclusive territory sounds attractive until you realize the commitment they want in return. If the market shifts or your volume doesn't grow as projected, you're locked into terms that don't work for you anymore.

Make sure the supplier's return policy actually works with eBay's requirements. If eBay forces a refund on a return case and your supplier won't accept the product back, you're eating the cost. There's no way to pass that loss upstream once the case is decided.

Get a price change notice period in writing. Suppliers who can adjust pricing with 24 hours notice can make profitable products unprofitable overnight while you still have active listings at the old margin. A 30-day notice clause gives you time to reprice or delist before the damage is done.

Spell out shipping time expectations in any formal agreement. "We ship within 2 business days" means something very different from "orders typically ship within 2 business days." The second version gives them cover to miss that window regularly without being in breach of anything.

> ■ **Danger Zone:** Never sign exclusive agreements or commit to minimum orders until you've thoroughly tested supplier performance and verified their ability to meet your business requirements.

Avoiding Common Supplier Pitfalls

Most supplier relationship failures follow the same patterns. Knowing them in advance doesn't prevent all of them, but it helps you recognize what's happening faster and respond before the damage accumulates.

Bait-and-switch pricing is common. The introductory rate gets you invested — you build listings, optimize titles, get some sales history — and then prices go up. Switching costs feel high at that point, which is exactly what they're counting on. The defense is to not become so dependent on a single supplier that a price increase locks you in.

Quality drift is harder to catch than a sudden price change. Products that were fine six months ago quietly get cheaper components, thinner packaging, or lower assembly standards. Buyers notice before you do, and by the time the negative feedback pattern is clear, the damage is already done. Periodic spot-checking, ordering and inspecting items yourself, is the only reliable early warning system.

Inventory availability is more volatile than suppliers usually admit. A supplier who carries a product does not necessarily have it in stock at all times. Overselling — when they sell to more dropshippers than they can fulfill — creates orders you can't ship and buyers who have to be cancelled. Real-time stock data integration is the fix; manually checking periodically is not.

Some suppliers go quiet after winning your business. They were responsive during the evaluation phase and now take days to answer questions. This usually reflects their actual service capacity rather than a temporary busy period. If communication is slow when there's no crisis, it will be worse when there is one.

Suppliers change their terms. Sometimes with notice, sometimes without. A policy that works for your business today may not work six months from now. Keep enough supplier relationships active that a single policy change doesn't force you to accept bad terms or shut down operations while you find an alternative.

Technology Integration and Automation

Managing supplier relationships manually across more than two or three sources becomes untenable fast. Once you're dealing with multiple suppliers, different product catalogs, varying stock feeds, and separate order forwarding processes, a centralized system isn't optional — it's what keeps you from making mistakes that cost real money.

API connections between your supplier and your eBay listings handle inventory updates and order forwarding automatically. Without them, every stock change requires a manual listing update, and every order requires manually copying a buyer's address into a supplier portal. At low volume that's manageable. At real volume it's where things break.

Inventory management tools that pull live stock data from your suppliers and automatically adjust or end listings when items go out of stock are the single most important protection against overselling. If you're not running one, you're relying on luck and manual checking to prevent a category of problem that happens regularly.

Track supplier performance in a dashboard you actually look at. Delivery times, order accuracy, return rates per supplier — these numbers tell you which relationships are working and which are quietly creating problems in your metrics before buyers tell you directly.

Keep records of every supplier communication. When a dispute arises, and it will, having a documented history of what was agreed, what was promised, and when problems were reported makes resolution faster and gives you standing if you need to escalate.

Finding good suppliers is hard work, and keeping them performing well is ongoing work. There's no point in the relationship where you can stop paying attention. The ones who treat it as a set-and-forget operation eventually discover why it isn't.

Dropshipping makes you a middleman juggling customer expectations, supplier limitations, and eBay's performance requirements while maintaining the illusion that you actually control the fulfillment process. Every order becomes a potential disaster where supplier mistakes become your customer service problems and delivery delays turn into negative feedback that destroys your seller metrics.

Order Processing Workflow Development

Every dropship order is a relay race where you're standing in the middle handing batons between a buyer who doesn't know your supplier exists and a supplier who doesn't care about your seller metrics. The moment an order comes in, your job is to move it through that handoff without anything getting dropped.

Acknowledge orders quickly. An automated order confirmation that goes out within minutes of purchase sets a professional tone and starts your eBay response time clock in a favorable direction. Buyers who hear nothing after purchasing start wondering whether their order registered — and wondering turns into messages, which turn into time spent on something that could have been handled automatically.

Forward orders to your supplier the same day. Every hour of delay here becomes a day of delay at the other end. Include the full buyer address, any special instructions, and a clear indication of which product and variant was ordered. Errors in this transmission are errors that show up in a buyer's mailbox two weeks later, and by then fixing them is expensive.

Before the order goes out the door, do a quick verification: does the address look complete? Is the product still in stock? Are there any flags in the order that suggest something might go wrong? Two minutes of checking here prevents two hours of damage control later.

Track every order from the moment it leaves your supplier until it arrives at the buyer's door. Not because you can intervene once it's in transit, but because you need to know when something has gone quiet — a shipment that hasn't moved in five days, a tracking number that was never scanned — before the buyer contacts you about it.

★ **Pro Tip:** Create automated email templates for each stage of order processing to maintain consistent customer communication while reducing the time investment required for routine order management.

Inventory Synchronization and Availability Management

Overselling is one of the most common ways dropshipping operations damage eBay accounts. A buyer purchases something you no longer have access to, you can't fulfill, you have to cancel — and eBay treats that cancelled transaction as a defect on your record. Enough of them and your account is on restricted status.

Real-time inventory feeds from your supplier directly into your eBay listings are the only reliable protection against this. Manual checking — even if you do it twice a day — leaves gaps. A supplier that sells out of something at 11pm won't show as out of stock in your listing until you check in the morning. By then you may have taken an order you can't fill.

Watch for seasonal depletion patterns and supplier discontinuation notices. Products that sell well in November can go out of stock permanently by December. If your supplier sends any kind of inventory notices, pay attention to them — and if they don't, build that into how you evaluate the relationship.

Even with live feeds, build in a buffer. If your supplier shows 3 units available, don't list 3. Other dropshippers may be drawing from the same pool. List what you can reasonably guarantee and end the listing before the last unit rather than racing to fulfill the final order.

Know what you'll do when something sells out mid-order. Do you have a comparable alternative from a different supplier? Can you source it quickly elsewhere? Having a plan before the crisis means a phone call instead of a cancelled transaction.

End listings fast when stock disappears. A listing with no available inventory sitting live on eBay is just waiting to take an order you can't fill. Automate the takedown if you can; manual processes have too many gaps.

Customer Communication and Expectation Management

The biggest customer service challenge in dropshipping is that you're answering for things you don't control. When a buyer asks where their package is, you're dependent on your supplier's tracking. When they ask why delivery is taking so long, the honest answer may involve a factory in another country — which is not the answer they want to hear. Managing this gap between what you promise and what you can actually deliver is most of what dropship customer service actually is.

Set accurate shipping timelines in your listings — not optimistic ones. If your supplier takes 3–4 weeks to deliver, say so. Buyers who choose to purchase knowing the timeline are far less likely to open cases than buyers who expected two days and got three weeks. The listing that sets honest expectations converts less often but generates fewer problems.

Get tracking numbers from your supplier the moment they ship and upload them to eBay immediately. This is not optional. It protects you legally in the event of an "item not received" claim, it satisfies buyers who check order status, and it improves the seller metrics eBay tracks for upload timing.

If a shipment is running late, reach out to the buyer before they reach out to you. A brief message saying you've noticed a delay and are following up with your supplier lands completely differently than a response to an angry message about a missing package. The first feels like service. The second feels like damage control.

Know your escalation path before you need it. When a buyer opens a case and you need answers from your supplier fast, you can't be figuring out who to contact. Have a direct contact at the supplier for urgent issues — not just a general support email — and know what information they need to resolve a dispute quickly.

Update buyers when something significant changes — not constantly, but when there's actually something to say. A message that says "your order shipped today" is useful. Daily "checking in" messages that contain no new information create noise and do not improve satisfaction.

> ▲ **Caution:** Never promise delivery dates you can't guarantee when working with third-party suppliers. Overcommitting on delivery times creates customer service disasters and negative feedback.

Quality Control and Inspection Processes

You can't inspect items before they ship to buyers. That's one of the fundamental trade-offs of dropshipping, and there's no workaround that fully compensates for it. What you can do is catch quality problems early — before they accumulate into a pattern that's visible in your feedback and your metrics.

Be explicit with your supplier about your quality and packaging expectations. Document it in writing. This doesn't guarantee they'll meet them, nothing does, but it gives you standing to push back when they don't, and it makes the expectations concrete rather than assumed.

Read every piece of buyer feedback and look for patterns. A single complaint about packaging might be bad luck. Three complaints about the same issue in a month is a supplier problem. Buyer feedback is your quality control data — it's just delayed and comes with a cost attached.

Track return rates by supplier and by product. A return rate above 5–8% on a specific item is a signal that something is wrong — either the listing description doesn't match the product, or the product itself doesn't meet buyer expectations. Either way, it needs to be fixed or the item needs to come down.

Verify that your listing photos accurately represent what's actually being shipped. This sounds basic, but supplier photo libraries often lag behind product changes. If the supplier updated the product but not the photos, your buyers are ordering based on something they won't receive.

Order samples periodically — not just when you start a supplier relationship, but every few months. Quality drift is real and subtle. Catching it on a sample order you pay for is much cheaper than catching it through buyer complaints and account metrics damage.

Return and Refund Coordination

Returns in dropshipping involve three parties: you, your supplier, and the buyer. The buyer only sees you. Whatever your supplier does or doesn't do, the buyer's experience is determined by how you handle it. eBay will back the buyer in most disputes if the process isn't handled correctly, so having a clear, fast return process isn't just good service — it's account protection.

Document your return process before you need it. When a return request comes in, you should already know: does the item go back to you or to the supplier? Who pays for return shipping in different scenarios? What information do you need from the buyer? A process you're inventing under pressure while a buyer waits is a process that makes mistakes.

For low-value items, consider whether fighting a return with your supplier is worth the time. Chasing a $12 credit from an overseas supplier who's slow to respond while the buyer is waiting is often less efficient than just issuing the refund and updating your cost model for that product. Save your supplier escalation effort for items where the dollar amount justifies it.

Issue refunds within eBay's required timelines regardless of where you are in the supplier coordination process. If you're waiting to hear back from your supplier while the refund clock is ticking, issue the refund and sort out the supplier credit separately. Missing an eBay deadline to manage a supplier situation is a false economy.

Restocking fees and return shipping charges are sometimes available to you under eBay policy, but use them carefully. Applying them in every return situation creates friction and disputes that cost more in time than you recover in fees. Use them for clear cases of buyer error or abuse, not as a standard cost-recovery tool.

When items arrive damaged, photograph the buyer's report immediately, process the refund or replacement quickly, and then pursue your supplier for the credit. The buyer's situation gets resolved first. The supplier negotiation happens after. That sequence keeps your account clean even when suppliers are slow.

> ■ **Danger Zone:** Never authorize returns without understanding your supplier's return policies and your ability to recover costs from returned merchandise.

Performance Monitoring and Supplier Management

Review supplier performance weekly. Not because things change that fast, but because weekly review catches a slow decline before it becomes a visible problem in your metrics. A supplier whose on-time delivery rate has dropped from 95% to 80% over four weeks is already damaging your account. Monthly reviews show you the damage after the fact.

Track the metrics that actually matter: average delivery time, order accuracy rate, percentage of orders with tracking uploaded on time, and return rate by supplier. These four numbers tell you most of what you need to know about whether a supplier relationship is working.

Test your supplier's response time when you need something urgently. How fast do they respond to a problem report? How long does it take to get a credit for a damaged item? Slow support in normal conditions becomes catastrophic support in a crisis. Know this before you're depending on them in a dispute.

Look for trends in buyer feedback before they become obvious. Three buyers mentioning the same issue in the same month is a pattern. By the time that pattern is undeniable, it's already in your feedback score and potentially in your seller standing.

Calculate the real profitability of each supplier relationship regularly, not just the nominal margin. Include returns, customer service time, and any credits you weren't able to recover. A supplier that looks fine on gross margin can look very different when you account for everything else they cost you.

Give suppliers feedback on what's working and what isn't. Most suppliers don't have visibility into how their products perform once they leave the warehouse. Telling a supplier "this product has a 12% return rate because the size runs small" is information they may act on — and if they don't, it tells you something about the relationship.

Technology Solutions and Automation

The operational complexity of dropshipping — multiple suppliers, live inventory feeds, order forwarding, tracking uploads, performance monitoring — is genuinely difficult to manage manually beyond a small volume. The tools exist to handle most of it, and the cost of those tools is far less than the cost of the mistakes manual management produces.

An order management system that pulls orders from eBay, forwards them to suppliers, and uploads tracking back to eBay automatically is the foundation. Everything else — inventory synchronization, performance dashboards, communication automation — builds on top of that. Start with order management and add from there as volume justifies it.

Make sure your inventory synchronization is genuinely real-time, not batch updates. A system that syncs stock every four hours is four hours of exposure to overselling during that window. For high-volume operations or fast-moving products, that gap matters.

Automate your routine communications — order confirmations, shipping notifications, delivery follow-ups — and preserve your personal attention for anything that doesn't fit the template. The goal is to handle everything routine at scale while still having capacity to handle the difficult situations personally.

Run performance reports weekly. Delivery times by supplier, return rates by product, customer service response times — these numbers tell you whether the operation is working before buyers and eBay metrics tell you it isn't.

Dropship order management isn't glamorous work. It's coordination, verification, and problem-catching done consistently enough that problems stay small. The sellers who build reliable systems for it spend most of their time on things that grow the business. The ones who don't spend most of their time putting out fires.

Dropshipping fails in predictable ways. The failures aren't random bad luck — they follow patterns that repeat across thousands of accounts and get reported in the same seller forums month after month. Knowing the patterns doesn't make you immune, but it means you can see what's coming early enough to adjust rather than discovering the problem through a suspension notice or a month of losses.

Account Suspension and Policy Violations

The suspension risk in dropshipping isn't theoretical. eBay has gotten better at identifying policy violations, and the enforcement is fast and often irreversible. Most suspended dropshipping accounts weren't suspended for one obvious violation — they accumulated small compliance failures until a threshold was crossed and the account disappeared without the appeal process producing any useful result.

Don't let your supplier communicate with buyers under their own branding. eBay requires you to be the identified seller on every buyer-facing communication and every package. A box arriving with your supplier's name and logo on it instead of yours is a policy violation, full stop. Buyers who figure out they're dealing with a middleman also sometimes report it.

eBay doesn't distinguish between supplier-caused metrics failures and seller-caused ones. If your supplier ships slow, your late shipment rate goes up. If your supplier sends wrong items, your defect rate goes up. The account that gets suspended is yours, not theirs. Your metrics reflect your supplier's performance whether you like it or not.

Overpromising in listings is a fast path to violations. Listing a delivery window your supplier can't consistently meet, describing condition more favorably than it is, or claiming features the product doesn't have — these create the misrepresentation cases that generate bad feedback and eBay intervention simultaneously.

Retail arbitrage — buying something from Amazon or Walmart after a sale and having it shipped directly to the buyer — is explicitly prohibited. Buyers who receive Amazon boxes with Amazon receipts inside report it. eBay is aware of the pattern and has mechanisms to detect it. This is not a gray area.

> ★ **Pro Tip:** Review eBay's current dropshipping policies monthly and document your compliance procedures to protect against policy changes and enforcement actions.

Financial Disasters and Cash Flow Problems

The most common financial mistake in dropshipping is confusing revenue with profit. A seller doing $10,000 a month in sales sounds successful. A seller doing $10,000 a month while netting $200 after eBay fees, supplier costs, returns, and customer service time is running a business that pays less than minimum wage for the hours invested.

Do the full margin calculation before listing anything. Supplier cost plus eBay final value fee (12–15%) plus payment processing plus return rate cost plus customer service time. If you're not running these numbers for every product before you list it, you're essentially guessing whether the business is profitable.

Cash flow timing catches a lot of new dropshippers off guard. You pay the supplier when the order comes in. eBay pays you on a schedule that might be days or weeks later — and can be held longer if your account is new or has performance flags. In a busy week, you're floating dozens of orders before a dollar clears. If you don't have working capital to bridge that gap, you'll eventually find yourself unable to pay for orders you've already taken.

Returns from international suppliers are often economically irrational. When return shipping to China costs more than the item is worth, you absorb the loss. The "refund without return" option costs you the full item cost. Neither outcome leaves you whole, and if it happens frequently enough on a particular product, the business case for carrying it collapses entirely.

Currency risk is real for international suppliers. A product that costs you $8 today might cost $9.50 next month if exchange rates shift. Dropshipping margins are thin enough that a 10–15% currency move can erase the profit on a whole product line without anyone making a deliberate business decision to change anything.

Track your actual costs, all of them, for at least 90 days before concluding the model works. Supplier processing fees, wire transfer fees, platform subscription costs, packaging, your time — these add up. Many sellers discover their true profitability only after several months of careful tracking, and the number is usually lower than they expected.

> ▲ **Caution:** Track all costs associated with dropshipping operations for at least 90 days before assuming your business model is profitable. Hidden costs often emerge after initial optimistic calculations.

Supplier Relationship Failures

Your entire dropshipping operation rests on supplier relationships you don't control. Any single supplier can take your business down — not maliciously, often just through ordinary business failures — and unless you have redundancy built in, there's no safety net.

Suppliers disappear. Overseas operations close without notice — factory closures, financial problems, regulatory issues — and you find out when orders stop shipping and your supplier stops answering emails. You have active listings, buyers waiting, and no way to fulfill. Every one of those orders is a refund, a potential negative, and a defect on your account.

Quality deterioration is insidious because it's gradual. The product that was fine six months ago quietly gets cheaper components or lighter packaging. Buyers start mentioning it in feedback before you notice the pattern. By the time it's undeniable, there are already multiple negative reviews attached to a product you trusted.

Price increases after you've built listings around a supplier are a classic move. They get you invested — optimized titles, sales history, good metrics on those specific listings — then raise prices knowing that the switching cost is real. The defense is to never let one supplier control a majority of your inventory, and to always know who your backup option is before you need them.

Supplier communication goes cold. They were responsive during vetting, answered quickly for the first few months, and then gradually became slower and less helpful. By the time they stop responding to urgent messages entirely, you're already in trouble. Watch for declining response times as an early warning sign, not just an inconvenience.

Policy changes arrive without warning. Minimum order thresholds go up. Shipping methods change. Return policies tighten. A supplier who served your business model six months ago may not serve it today, and you may find out from a failed order rather than advance notice.

Stock data gets shared across many dropshippers. When a supplier sells to twenty resellers and shows "100 units available," that number is being drawn down by all twenty simultaneously. Overselling doesn't require your supplier to be dishonest — it just requires the stock to move faster than the feed updates.

Customer Service Nightmares

Every customer service problem in dropshipping has an extra layer: you have to solve it through a supplier who doesn't share your urgency, doesn't face your eBay consequences, and may be operating in a different time zone where your "urgent" message arrives at 2am their time.

A buyer waiting two weeks for something that was supposed to arrive in five days doesn't care why. They care when it's coming. If you can't answer that because your supplier hasn't responded, you're in the position of apologizing for a situation you can't resolve. Buyers in that position leave bad feedback. They open cases. They push eBay to intervene, and eBay usually sides with them.

Quality complaints are the worst version of this because they require your supplier to acknowledge a problem, which many are reluctant to do. While you're waiting for the supplier to confirm the product is defective so you can issue a refund in good conscience, the buyer's patience is running out and eBay's resolution clock is ticking.

International returns are often economically broken. A buyer wants to return a $20 item, the supplier requires it be shipped back to China, and the shipping cost exceeds the item value. You're left choosing between absorbing a full loss or fighting with a buyer over a return policy that technically applies but practically doesn't work.

Buyers sometimes find supplier contact information on packaging and reach out directly. They get different information than you gave them. Now you have a confused buyer who doesn't know what they were told, a supplier who doesn't know the full history of the case, and a mess to untangle that should never have happened. Your packaging should have no supplier contact information on it.

Language barriers with overseas suppliers slow everything down when problems need solving quickly. A supplier support rep who communicates primarily through translated responses that don't quite match your questions creates compounding delays in situations where days matter for keeping the buyer from escalating.

Small issues escalate to eBay cases faster in dropshipping than in inventory-based selling because you're slower to resolve them. Inventory sellers can often make a buyer whole within hours. Dropshippers are dependent on a third party, and that dependency shows in response times. Buyers who wait more than 24 hours for a meaningful resolution often just click "open a case" instead.

Market Saturation and Competition

This is the core problem with generic dropshipping in 2025: the market is already saturated for almost every mainstream product category. Temu, DHgate, and AliExpress-connected operations have automated the listing process to the point where a single operation can flood eBay with tens of thousands of identical products. You're not just competing with other dropshippers — you're competing with automation at industrial scale.

The price race to the bottom is not a risk in saturated categories — it's already happened. Search for almost any generic consumer product on eBay and you'll find dozens of identical listings competing on fractions of a dollar. The margin that might have existed two years ago was competed away when the barrier to entry dropped to near zero.

When fifty sellers list the same product with the same supplier photos, the only differentiator is price. Buyers sort by price. You're either the cheapest or you're not getting the sale. And the cheapest option is usually the overseas operation with no overhead, selling at a margin that makes no business sense for anyone paying their own bills.

eBay's algorithm favors sellers with established history, strong metrics, and good conversion rates. A new dropshipping account entering a saturated category starts at the back of the search results, competing against sellers who have years of positive feedback and sales velocity. Getting traction without that history requires either a niche where you can stand out or a marketing spend that erases the margins you were trying to protect.

High-volume operations get better treatment from suppliers — better prices, priority fulfillment, first access to new products.

Small dropshippers get standard pricing and standard service. The gap between what the biggest operations pay per unit and what you pay can make your product economically uncompetitive regardless of how well you run everything else.

Some suppliers sell directly on eBay and Amazon alongside their dropship partners. They have lower costs than you, faster shipping because they ship directly, and brand recognition you can't match. If your supplier is also your competitor, that's a structural problem with the relationship that no amount of operational efficiency fixes.

Legal and Compliance Risks

Most dropshippers don't think about legal exposure until something goes wrong. The legal reality is uncomplicated: you sold it, you're responsible for it. Where it was manufactured, who shipped it, whether you ever touched it — none of that insulates you from liability when a product causes harm.

Product liability follows the seller, not the manufacturer. A defective item that injures someone or causes property damage creates a claim against you, not the overseas factory. The factory may be unreachable, uninsured, and operating under a different legal system. You are none of those things. Avoid categories with safety risk — electronics, children's items, health products — unless you've verified certifications in writing.

International suppliers sometimes ship products that don't meet US safety standards, FDA requirements, or import restrictions — and they don't always disclose this. You find out when a shipment is held at customs, when a buyer complains about a product that doesn't comply with labeling requirements, or when a regulatory complaint lands on your account.

Check whether your state or jurisdiction requires any business registration or resale permits for the volume you're doing. Requirements vary, and "I didn't know" is not a defense. eBay reports income to the IRS and issues 1099s — your sales are visible.

eBay collects sales tax in most states automatically, which removes one compliance headache. But income tax on dropshipping profits is entirely your responsibility, and the self-employment considerations are more complex than a standard W-2. Get a tax professional who understands e-commerce before you're filing the first return.

Suppliers who use stolen product photos, counterfeit items, or trademark violations create intellectual property liability that lands on the seller, not the supplier. A brand protection complaint from a major trademark holder can result in listing removal, account action, and legal exposure. Verify that what you're listing is what the supplier actually has the right to sell.

Technology and Operational Failures

Dropshipping depends on software systems staying operational, and they don't always. Inventory feeds go down. Order management platforms have outages. API connections between eBay and your supplier fail without triggering any error message visible to you. Every one of these failure modes has the same consequence: orders you can't fulfill, buyers you can't update, and metrics damage accumulating in the background.

Inventory sync failures result in overselling. An item that went out of stock at your supplier is still showing as available in your listing because the feed hasn't updated. A buyer purchases it. Now you have to cancel the transaction, which counts as a defect. This happens most often during peak periods when suppliers are moving inventory fast and feed update intervals can't keep up.

Order forwarding errors send the wrong product or wrong address to your supplier. By the time the error surfaces — when the buyer receives something unexpected or nothing at all — the original ship window has passed and correcting it requires starting over. Automated systems reduce these errors, but they don't eliminate them, and no automated system catches 100% of edge cases.

Communication automation failures mean buyers don't get shipping notifications or delivery confirmations, which increases "where is my order" messages and creates the impression of poor service even when everything shipped fine. Monitor your automation to confirm it's actually firing, not just assume it is.

Third-party platform outages are outside your control, but their impact isn't. If your order management tool goes down during a busy weekend, you're processing orders manually — slowly, with more errors. Know what your manual fallback is before the outage happens, not during it.

Build redundancy into every critical system. Backup supplier for your main products. Manual order process documented and tested. Alternative communication channels if your primary system fails. The sellers who weather technology failures without damage are the ones who planned for them when nothing was wrong.

The fundamental thing that makes dropshipping harder than it looks is that every failure mode is amplified. When an inventory seller ships the wrong item, it's one mistake they fix directly. When a dropshipper's supplier ships the wrong item to twenty buyers, it's twenty simultaneous customer service fires and twenty simultaneous account metric hits. The leverage that makes dropshipping appealing — doing more volume without holding inventory — is exactly the same leverage that makes its failure modes so destructive.

None of this means it can't work. It means it requires better planning, more redundancy, and more realistic expectations than most people bring to it. The sellers who succeed at eBay dropshipping treat it as a serious business with serious operational requirements — not as a passive income stream that runs itself.

PART V: Protecting Your Business

Chapter 20: Common Scams and How to Avoid Them

eBay scams have gotten more sophisticated as the platform has grown. What used to be clumsy fraud attempts — fake payment emails that barely looked real, obvious overpayment schemes — have evolved into operations that use detailed knowledge of eBay's own policies against sellers. The most effective scams don't look like scams. They look like normal transactions that go slightly wrong in ways you didn't anticipate.

The common thread is that most scams exploit seller urgency, goodwill, or unfamiliarity with how disputes actually work. Knowing the patterns means you can recognize what's happening while there's still time to stop it — rather than discovering the problem after the item has shipped and the payment has reversed.

Fake Payment Confirmation Scams

Payment confirmation scams target sellers with sophisticated fake emails, doctored screenshots, and convincing stories about payment processing delays that trick sellers into shipping expensive items before payments clear through legitimate channels.

Scammers create fake PayPal emails that appear authentic but contain subtle differences in sender addresses, formatting, or language that reveal their fraudulent nature when examined carefully. These emails often claim payments are pending, held for review, or require additional verification before funds become available.

Screenshot manipulation involves altered images of payment confirmations, bank deposits, or money transfer receipts that look convincing but represent completely fabricated transactions. Modern photo editing software makes these fakes increasingly difficult to distinguish from legitimate payment documentation.

Pressure tactics create artificial urgency through stories about sick relatives, time-sensitive shipping requirements, or limited availability that pressure sellers into shipping items before payment verification can be completed through proper channels.

Email spoofing techniques make fraudulent messages appear to originate from legitimate financial institutions, eBay, or PayPal while actually coming from criminal operations designed to steal money and merchandise from unsuspecting sellers.

★ **Pro Tip:** Always verify payments through direct login to your payment processor's website, never through email links or screenshots provided by buyers.

Overpayment and Refund Scams

Overpayment scams involve buyers who send payments exceeding the purchase amount and request refunds for the difference, using stolen payment methods that will be reversed after sellers have already sent refund money and shipped merchandise.

Check overpayment represents a classic version where scammers send counterfeit cashier's checks for amounts exceeding purchase prices, requesting wire transfers or money orders for the difference before banks discover the fraudulent nature of the original payment.

Credit card overpayment occurs when scammers use stolen credit cards to make purchases exceeding item prices, then request refunds to different accounts before credit card companies discover the unauthorized transactions and reverse all payments.

International money transfer scams involve complex payment arrangements where scammers claim to send extra money to cover shipping, customs, or handling fees, then request refunds through untraceable transfer methods that disappear when original payments are reversed.

Shipping company payment schemes include offers to overpay for items while requesting sellers to forward excess payments to shipping companies or freight forwarders that exist only to collect fraudulent refund payments.

> ▲ **Caution:** Never accept payments exceeding your item prices, and never send refunds until payments have completely cleared through your financial institutions.

Phishing and Account Takeover Attempts

Phishing scams use sophisticated fake websites and emails that mimic eBay, PayPal, and other legitimate services to steal login credentials that enable account takeovers and financial theft from unsuspecting sellers.

Fake eBay websites replicate the platform's appearance with subtle URL differences that trick sellers into entering usernames and passwords on criminal-controlled servers that capture login information for later misuse.

Email phishing campaigns send messages claiming account problems, policy violations, or security issues that require immediate login through provided links that lead to fake websites designed to steal authentication credentials.

Phone phishing involves callers claiming to represent eBay, PayPal, or financial institutions who request account information, passwords, or verification codes under pretenses of security checks or problem resolution.

Two-factor authentication bypass attempts involve sophisticated social engineering designed to obtain authentication codes that enable account access despite security measures intended to prevent unauthorized login attempts.

Password reset exploitation uses publicly available personal information to answer security questions or trick customer service representatives into providing account access to criminals who impersonate legitimate account holders.

Shipping and Address Manipulation Frauds

Shipping fraud involves elaborate schemes designed to steal merchandise while creating apparent proof of delivery that protects scammers from dispute resolution and chargeback procedures.

Address forwarding scams begin with legitimate shipping addresses that get changed after sellers create shipping labels, redirecting packages to criminal addresses while maintaining tracking information that suggests proper delivery.

Intercepted package fraud involves scammers who monitor tracking information and intercept deliveries through fake identification, forged signatures, or mail theft that occurs before legitimate recipients receive their merchandise.

False delivery confirmation occurs when criminals sign for packages using fake names or forge signatures that create tracking records suggesting successful delivery while actual recipients never receive their purchases.

Shipping company collusion involves corrupt employees at shipping companies who assist scammers by confirming false deliveries, redirecting packages, or providing tracking information that supports fraudulent claims about completed shipments.

> ■ **Danger Zone:** Always require signature confirmation for higher-value items and verify recipient identity matches buyer information before considering deliveries complete.

Return Scam Variations

Return scams exploit eBay's buyer-friendly return policies to obtain free merchandise, partial refunds, or replacement items through fraudulent claims about product condition, delivery issues, or seller misrepresentation.

Bait and switch returns involve buyers who return different items than they purchased, counting on sellers not to notice substitutions of similar but less valuable products or damaged merchandise.

Empty box returns occur when scammers return packages containing worthless items while claiming to return original merchandise, often using weighted boxes that feel correct during initial inspection.

Partial return fraud involves claims about missing components, accessories, or product portions that enable buyers to keep valuable parts while obtaining partial refunds for allegedly incomplete shipments.

Damage claim manipulation includes buyers who intentionally damage items after delivery, then claim products arrived in poor condition to obtain refunds while keeping damaged but still usable merchandise.

Serial return abuse involves buyers who systematically purchase items, use them temporarily, then return them with fabricated complaints designed to obtain free temporary product usage.

Fake Buyer and Bidding Scams

Fake buyer scams involve non-existent purchasers who win auctions or commit to purchases with no intention of completing transactions, wasting seller time while potentially manipulating market prices or gathering business intelligence.

Shill bidding involves fake bidders who artificially inflate auction prices to help accomplices win items at higher costs or manipulate market perceptions about item values for future sales opportunities.

Information gathering scams use fake purchase inquiries to obtain detailed product information, photos, or business intelligence that competitors or criminals use for unauthorized purposes.

Auction manipulation involves coordinated bidding designed to influence final sale prices, either to inflate values artificially or make sure accomplices win items at predetermined prices that benefit criminal operations.

Time-wasting strategies keep sellers engaged in lengthy communications about fake purchases while scammers gather information or prevent items from being sold to legitimate buyers during peak demand periods.

Business Opportunity and Service Scams

Business opportunity scams target successful sellers with offers for inventory, services, or partnerships designed to steal money, merchandise, or business information from entrepreneurs seeking growth opportunities.

Fake supplier schemes promise access to exclusive products, wholesale pricing, or dropshipping opportunities that require upfront payments for membership fees, sample orders, or business setup costs that never deliver promised benefits.

Service provider fraud involves companies offering eBay store design, listing optimization, or business consulting services that disappear after collecting payment without delivering promised work or results.

Partnership proposals from fake investors or business partners who request financial information, inventory access, or account privileges that enable theft of money, merchandise, or business assets.

Software and automation scams promise miraculous results from expensive programs that automate eBay selling, optimize listings, or generate profits through secret strategies that don't work as advertised.

Protection Strategies and Best Practices

Effective scam protection requires combining technological safeguards with behavioral awareness and verification procedures that make criminal targeting unprofitable and unsuccessful.

Verification procedures should include confirming buyer identity, validating payment methods, and checking shipping addresses against known fraud databases before committing to high-value transactions.

Communication red flags include poor grammar, urgent deadlines, overly generous terms, requests for personal information, or payment arrangements that deviate from standard eBay procedures.

Documentation practices help protect against false claims by maintaining detailed records of all communications, transaction details, shipping information, and product condition evidence.

Technology safeguards include using secure networks, enabling two-factor authentication, keeping software updated, and avoiding suspicious links or downloads that could compromise account security.

Professional skepticism helps evaluate offers, requests, and opportunities that seem too good to be true or deviate from normal business patterns in ways that benefit unknown parties more than yourself.

Problem buyers on eBay range from genuinely confused customers who need patient education to professional scammers who target sellers with elaborate fraud schemes designed to steal merchandise and money. Modern eBay's buyer-centric policies have emboldened difficult customers who understand they hold most of the power in disputes and can weaponize feedback threats to extract undeserved concessions from sellers.

Dealing with problem buyers starts with telling the difference between legitimate customer concerns and manipulation attempts. eBay's policy framework heavily favors buyer satisfaction, which means your instinct to be right matters less than your ability to resolve things quickly and cheaply.

Identifying Problem Buyer Types

Most problem buyers fall into one of a handful of recognizable patterns. Knowing which type you're dealing with early changes how you respond — and how much energy you spend on it.

Confused buyers are more common than any other type and the least actually problematic. They misread a description, misunderstood shipping time, or aren't sure how eBay works. They're annoying because they generate messages that take time, but they're usually satisfied by a clear, patient explanation. Most of the time they leave positive feedback once someone took the time to help them.

Demanding buyers know what they want and won't let you forget it. They expect immediate responses, perfect service, and some accommodation for every minor inconvenience. They're exhausting but usually legitimate. The ones who threaten feedback over every small imperfection are testing whether you'll cave. Set a clear, polite boundary once — "here's what I can do" — and hold it.

Serial returners use eBay's return policies as a rental program. They buy, use, and return — often with fabricated complaints to avoid questions. The telltale sign is a buyer with a return history on their account, or someone whose complaints are inconsistent with how you described and photographed the item. Block them after the first occurrence; they'll keep coming back if you don't.

Scammers are a different animal entirely — organized, often running multiple accounts, and using specific techniques that work because most sellers haven't seen them before. False "item not received" claims on items with confirmed delivery, swapping out defective items for working ones then claiming the working one was defective, or payment reversal schemes after item has shipped. Chapter 20 covers the specific techniques in detail.

Feedback extortionists are the most infuriating category because eBay's platform structure gives them real leverage. They know negative feedback hurts your metrics and that most sellers would rather give a small refund than fight it. The message pattern is usually "I'm not happy and I'm thinking about leaving feedback — unless...". This is policy-violating behavior, but getting eBay to remove the feedback requires documentation and effort that many sellers don't bother with.

> ★ **Pro Tip:** Document all interactions with difficult buyers to build evidence files that support your position if disputes escalate to eBay case resolution or feedback removal requests.

Early Warning Signs and Red Flags

Most problem buyers signal what's coming before the transaction is complete. The signals aren't always obvious, but they're usually there.

Watch the tone of pre-sale messages. A buyer who's aggressive or demanding before they've even purchased will be more so after. Someone who asks three different ways whether they can return the item if they change their mind is probably planning to. These aren't guarantees — some genuinely anxious buyers are great customers — but they're worth noting.

Check buyer feedback and account age for high-value transactions. A zero-feedback account buying a $500 item deserves extra documentation — more detailed photos before shipping, extra care with the tracking upload. New accounts belong to new buyers, but they also belong to previously banned buyers who created fresh accounts to continue whatever got them banned.

Shipping address oddities are worth a second look. A buyer registered in Florida requesting delivery to a freight forwarder in New Jersey isn't automatically fraudulent, but it's worth confirming the address before shipping expensive items. Freight forwarders complicate dispute resolution because eBay's buyer protection often ends at the confirmed delivery point, which may be a warehouse the buyer never sees.

eBay's managed payments means actual payment irregularities are less common than they used to be, but requests to pay outside eBay — PayPal friends and family, Zelle, wire transfer — are scams. Always. No exceptions. The moment someone suggests an off-platform payment method, the transaction is over.

Pre-purchase questions focused heavily on return policies and dispute processes, rather than the item itself, suggest someone who's already thinking about how to reverse the transaction. Most genuine buyers ask about the item. Buyers who ask extensively about what happens if something goes wrong are often planning for something to go wrong.

Artificial urgency before the sale — "I need this shipped today or I'll have to cancel" — is pressure designed to make you skip your normal procedures. Scammers use urgency to rush sellers into shipping before documentation is complete or verification is done. Normal buyers can wait your standard handling time.

Professional Communication Strategies

The single most important rule for communicating with problem buyers is to stay calm and stay factual. Emotional responses — frustration, defensiveness, sarcasm — give buyers ammunition and make you look bad if eBay reviews the conversation. Professional, neutral, and factual wins every time, even when the buyer is being unreasonable.

Document everything through eBay's messaging system. Screenshot communications that happen outside of it. If a dispute goes to eBay for resolution, your message history is evidence. A buyer claiming an item wasn't described accurately has a much harder case when you can show the eBay thread where you answered their questions about condition in detail before they bought.

Set your position clearly once, then hold it. "Based on your description, here's what I'm able to offer: X. If that doesn't work for you, you can open a return request through eBay's system." That's the message. Repeating it calmly is fine. Negotiating it away piece by piece because someone keeps pushing is not — it signals that persistence pays off.

When a buyer is genuinely frustrated but has a legitimate concern, acknowledge it directly before explaining your position. "I understand this isn't what you expected" costs nothing and often defuses situations before they escalate. Buyers who feel heard are less likely to reach for eBay's dispute button.

Don't take the bait when buyers try to provoke an emotional response. A message that accuses you of being a scammer or threatens to ruin your store is designed to make you react. A calm, factual response — or no response if there's nothing substantive to address — leaves them with nothing to use against you.

Keep everything in writing. Phone calls and voice messages aren't documented and can't be submitted to eBay. If a buyer insists on calling, follow up with a message summarizing what was discussed. That written summary becomes the record, not the conversation.

> ▲ **Caution:** Never engage in arguments or emotional responses with difficult buyers. Professional communication protects you legally and helps maintain your seller standing during disputes.

Dispute Prevention and Management

Most eBay disputes are preventable. Not all — some buyers are going to open cases regardless — but the majority happen because a seller was slow to respond, vague about their policy, or unwilling to deal with the problem early when a small concession would have resolved it.

If you can see a problem developing — a complaint message, a confused question, any signal that a buyer is unhappy — address it before they click "open a case." A partial refund offered proactively costs less than a full refund plus a defect on your account. A replacement shipped immediately costs less than a dispute resolved in the buyer's favor. Getting ahead of the problem is almost always the better financial decision.

Know your policies and apply them consistently. Inconsistency is exploitable — a buyer who knows you made an exception for someone else will expect one too. But also know when to make exceptions. Rigid policy enforcement on a clearly legitimate problem creates a dispute. The question isn't "what does my policy say" — it's "what's the cheapest way to make this buyer happy and protect my account?"

Document as you go. Photograph items before shipping, especially anything valuable or condition-sensitive. Keep tracking information. Save communication. If a dispute does happen, your evidence determines the outcome more than your argument does. eBay reviews documentation, not persuasiveness.

When a case does open, respond quickly and completely. eBay's system gives sellers a window to respond before cases escalate. Missing that window — or responding with incomplete information — often results in an automatic ruling for the buyer.

The speed and quality of your first response matters more than most sellers realize.

Negotiating directly with the buyer before a case goes to eBay often produces better outcomes. A buyer who got a partial refund and felt heard is less likely to leave bad feedback than one who went through a formal dispute process even if they "won." The formal process adds friction, stress, and sometimes spite to an already difficult situation.

Return Abuse and Serial Returners

Return abuse is one of the more expensive problems in eBay selling and one of the hardest to fight, because eBay's default stance is pro-buyer in return disputes. The platform's policies assume good faith from buyers, which serial abusers exploit systematically.

Look at buyer history before accepting returns on high-value items. A buyer with multiple returns across different sellers in a short period is running a pattern. eBay doesn't always make this information easy to find, but feedback left for that buyer by other sellers sometimes reveals the pattern even when the numbers don't.

When a return comes in, inspect the item before issuing the refund. Compare it against your pre-shipping photos. Items returned in different condition than shipped — switched for a defective unit, damaged during use, or simply not the item you sent — give you grounds to dispute the return. Document the discrepancy with photos immediately on receipt. That documentation is what you submit to eBay when you dispute.

Restocking fees are available in limited circumstances under eBay policy — mainly for buyer remorse returns where the item is returned in original condition. They're not available for returns where eBay decides the item wasn't as described. Know when you can apply them and when you can't; applying them incorrectly creates a dispute you'll lose.

Block buyers who abuse returns. eBay provides a buyer block list for this reason. A buyer who returned an item with a fabricated complaint once will do it again. There's no upside to leaving them unblocked — you gain nothing from their future purchases and risk another expensive return.

Apply your return policy consistently, but use your judgment on edge cases. A buyer who purchased something six months ago and is returning it now deserves a different response than one returning a week-old item with a legitimate complaint. eBay's formal policies set floors — you can be more generous when it makes sense, and more firm when abuse is clear.

> ■ **Danger Zone:** Never automatically accept all return requests without verification. Return abuse can destroy profitability faster than any other single factor in eBay selling.

Feedback Extortion and Threats

Feedback extortion is when a buyer threatens to leave negative feedback unless you give them something they're not entitled to. It's against eBay's policies and also frustratingly common. The platform's policies make it hard to remove retaliatory feedback even when the extortion is obvious, so the fight is often more expensive than just paying the ransom — which is exactly why it works.

The pattern is usually clear: "I'm not satisfied and I'm going to leave negative feedback unless you refund me / give me a discount / send a replacement for free." Sometimes it's more subtle — "I really don't want to have to leave bad feedback" — but the implicit threat is the same. Once you recognize it, screenshot the message. That screenshot is your evidence for a feedback removal request.

If you want to request feedback removal, you need the explicit threat documented, a timeline showing the sequence, and a clear explanation to eBay of why the feedback is retaliatory. eBay doesn't make this process easy and doesn't always rule in the seller's favor even with clear evidence. Going in with realistic expectations about success rate saves frustration.

Whether to accommodate an extortion attempt is a judgment call based on the cost. A buyer threatening bad feedback over a $15 item might not be worth fighting — refund and block them. A buyer threatening bad feedback after a $200 transaction needs a different calculation. What's the negative feedback actually going to cost you in visibility and lost sales versus the cost of the concession? That answer is different for every seller and every situation.

Opening a formal eBay case when extortion happens creates an official record. It signals to eBay that something abnormal is going on and can support your feedback removal request later. It also sometimes prompts eBay to contact the buyer directly, which occasionally resolves the situation without you having to capitulate.

The best long-term defense against extortion is not caving to it. Sellers with a reputation for accommodating threats attract more threats. If your policies are clear, your listings are accurate, and you respond to legitimate issues fairly, most extortion attempts have no real leverage — because there's no genuine grievance to threaten with.

Legal Considerations and Protection

Most problem buyer situations stay within eBay's dispute resolution system, which is the appropriate place to resolve them. But some cross lines that create actual legal exposure — fraud, theft of merchandise, harassment — and it's worth knowing what options exist beyond eBay's appeals process.

Your terms and conditions in the listing are a form of contract. Clear, specific policies — return windows, condition standards, what qualifies for a refund — create documented expectations that support your position in disputes. Vague or nonexistent policies leave you arguing from a weaker position when a buyer claims the transaction didn't meet their expectations.

If your business reaches a scale where individual disputes could represent significant losses, look into business insurance that covers e-commerce transactions. Most small sellers don't need it, but sellers handling high-value goods or large volumes face more exposure than personal liability alone covers.

Keep records of every significant transaction: the listing, the photos, the communications, the tracking. These records don't just support eBay disputes — they support your position if a situation ever requires a demand letter or a small claims filing. Records you don't have are arguments you can't make.

Small claims court is a realistic option when a buyer refuses to return an item after receiving a refund, makes provably false claims that result in a financial loss, or causes damages eBay's system won't cover. The threshold varies by state but is generally in the range of $5,000–$10,000. It's rarely worth it for small amounts, but for significant losses it's an option most buyers aren't expecting.

When financial losses are significant, potential fraud is involved, or a situation starts looking like criminal activity — coordinated buyer rings, identity theft — talk to a lawyer. Not every problem needs one, but when it does, having established the relationship in advance is better than finding one in a crisis.

System-Level Protection Strategies

Individual problem buyers are manageable. A business that keeps attracting them has a systemic issue — unclear listings, inaccurate condition descriptions, unrealistic shipping promises — that's generating friction across multiple transactions. High dispute rates are usually a signal about your listings or your processes, not just about unlucky buyer selection.

Use eBay's buyer requirements settings to filter out high-risk buyers before they purchase. You can block buyers with recent policy violations, buyers from countries you don't ship to, and buyers with unpaid item strikes. These filters don't catch everyone, but they remove the most obvious candidates for problems.

Response time templates handle routine inquiries fast while freeing up your attention for the situations that actually need it.

A buyer who gets a quick, clear answer to a standard question rarely escalates. A buyer who waits two days for a response has already gotten frustrated enough to consider other options.

Know your escalation path before you need it. When a situation goes beyond normal customer service — suspected fraud, escalating harassment, significant financial loss — you need to know the next step without figuring it out under pressure. eBay case filing, feedback removal request, buyer block, small claims — these are the steps in roughly that order, and knowing them in advance keeps you from making reactive decisions.

Track your dispute rate and feedback comments over time. If the same complaint keeps appearing — "item not as described," "slower than expected," "condition worse than listed" — that's a listing problem, not a buyer problem. Fix the listing and the complaints often stop.

Problem buyers are an occupational hazard. Sellers who stay in business long enough encounter every type eventually. What separates the ones who handle it well from the ones who burn out over it is treating difficult transactions as process problems to solve rather than personal affronts to endure. Keep your documentation current, your responses professional, and your policies clear — and most of the difficult situations resolve without escalating to something that actually damages the business.

eBay policy violations will end your account faster than anything else you can do wrong as a seller. The platform's enforcement systems are automated and aggressive, and the appeals process offers limited relief. Understanding the most common violations isn't a compliance exercise — it's the difference between a business that keeps running and one that disappears without much recourse.

Most violations fall into predictable categories. Most are avoidable if you know what to watch for. The ones that destroy accounts fastest are usually the ones sellers assumed weren't a big deal until they were.

Intellectual Property and Trademark Violations

IP violations are among the fastest paths to suspension because major brands actively monitor eBay for unauthorized use of their marks and images. They use automated tools. They file complaints in volume. eBay's response is to remove first and sort it out later — which means your listing is gone before you know there was a problem.

Counterfeit sales are treated as the most serious category of violation — immediate suspension, no warning, and the potential for criminal liability beyond just account loss. eBay holds you responsible regardless of what your supplier told you. If a supplier's prices for branded goods seem implausibly low, that's your signal. Verify authenticity before you list, not after a complaint arrives.

Selling genuine branded products is generally legal under first sale doctrine. Where it gets complicated is using brand names in your title when the item isn't that brand — even for comparison or compatibility purposes. "Fits Nike Air Jordan" in a title for a non-Nike product can trigger a trademark complaint. "Compatible with iPhone" for a third-party cable is generally fine; "iPhone-style case" for a generic product is not.

Using manufacturer photos is copyright infringement whether or not you know the image is protected. Most product images belong to manufacturers or retailers who did not give you permission to use them. Take your own photos. This protects you from DMCA takedowns, makes your listing look more authentic, and is one of the simplest things you can do to reduce IP risk.

Keyword stuffing brand names into titles or descriptions to attract search traffic — even for items where the brand is genuinely related — can still trigger violations when eBay's system determines the mentions are there for traffic manipulation rather than accurate description. Keep brand mentions factual and directly relevant to what you're actually selling.

> ★ **Pro Tip:** When in doubt about IP rights, take your own photos and write your own descriptions. That eliminates two of the three most common IP violation triggers in a single step.

Prohibited and Restricted Items

eBay's prohibited and restricted items list is long, changes without much notice, and contains some surprises for sellers who assume that legal-to-own means legal-to-list. Before you list anything in a category you haven't sold in before, check the policy page. The items that get sellers in trouble most often aren't the obvious ones — they're the edge cases nobody thought to look up.

Weapons and weapon accessories have restrictions that go well beyond firearms. Certain folding knives, brass knuckles, martial arts weapons, and replica guns are restricted even where ownership is legal. The test isn't whether you can own it — it's whether eBay allows it to be listed.

Health and medical items are heavily regulated. Prescription drugs are prohibited entirely. Many over-the-counter medications require age verification or have quantity limits. Medical devices that require a practitioner are restricted.

Electronics with specific radio frequencies — signal jammers, certain drones — have FCC-based restrictions that eBay enforces. Hazardous materials including flammables, pressurized containers, and certain chemicals are prohibited from shipping, making listing them a violation regardless of how you handle fulfillment.

> ▲ **Caution:** Items that were allowed last year may not be allowed today. eBay updates prohibited item lists without grandfathering active listings — a listing that existed before a policy change can still be removed and count against you.

Listing Policy Violations

Most listing violations aren't malicious — they're mistakes, old habits, or practices that were acceptable before a policy changed. eBay's automated systems don't distinguish between intentional violations and innocent errors. Either way, the listing gets removed and the violation counts against you.

Keyword spamming — putting brand names or search terms in your title that don't describe what you're selling — is a policy violation even when done to catch related searches. Describe what you have accurately. Category misplacement to avoid fees or gain visibility is detected and leads to removal and escalating restrictions with repetition.

Condition misrepresentation is one of the most direct paths to "not as described" returns and defect accumulation. Describe what you're actually selling, including the flaws. Photos of the actual item are required — stock photos and manufacturer images are policy violations. Take photos of the specific item you're listing. Title formatting prohibits excessive caps, decorative special characters, and promotional language that doesn't describe the item.

Fee Avoidance and Payment Violations

Fee avoidance is treated as one of the most serious violations because it directly attacks eBay's business model. Any attempt to complete a transaction outside eBay's payment system, or to steer buyers toward off-platform contact to avoid fees, can result in permanent account termination. This includes sharing contact information in buyer messages, suggesting alternative payment methods, or arranging local pickup outside the platform's transaction process.

Shill bidding — using another account or having someone bid on your auctions to drive prices up — is fraud. eBay's systems detect bid patterns consistent with shill activity, and the penalties include permanent bans for all associated accounts. The detection is better than most sellers assume.

> ■ **Danger Zone:** Never attempt to complete transactions outside eBay's payment system. Even suggesting it in a message to a buyer can result in permanent suspension — eBay treats it as a direct threat to their revenue.

Performance Standard Violations

Performance violations accumulate rather than detonate. Late shipments add up. Cases closed without resolution add up. Returns above category thresholds add up. Each one is a small negative metric event, and when the cumulative picture crosses eBay's thresholds, restrictions and suspension follow automatically without requiring a specific incident.

The most common cause of late shipment defects isn't late shipping — it's late tracking uploads. Carriers scan packages late sometimes. eBay counts the scan as your shipment date. Upload tracking immediately when you create the label. High return rates on a specific item almost always mean the listing doesn't match what buyers receive. Find that gap and close it.

Communication and Contact Information Violations

eBay treats almost any attempt to move buyer communication off-platform as a potential fee avoidance attempt. Sharing your email, phone number, or social media handle in a buyer message, even for innocent reasons, can trigger a policy violation. Listings can't include links to outside websites or social media. Using eBay's messaging system to promote other products or send marketing content unrelated to the specific transaction is prohibited. Keep communication transactional.

Account Security and Misuse Violations

Running multiple accounts without authorization is detected through IP patterns, payment information, device fingerprinting, and linked account relationships. All connected accounts get suspended, not just the unauthorized one. If you have a legitimate need for multiple accounts, get explicit eBay approval first. Account sharing — letting someone else log into your account — creates liability for everything that person does on your account. Use eBay's official multi-user tools instead.

Banned sellers who create new accounts are discovered through the same pattern-matching that caught them initially — shared IP addresses, bank accounts, device identifiers, addresses. The new account doesn't provide a fresh start; it just adds a second violation.

Staying Current with Policy Changes

eBay changes policies frequently and doesn't always send targeted notifications to sellers whose practices are about to become violations. You're responsible for knowing the current rules regardless of whether you were notified. Read the seller announcement emails instead of deleting them. Check the seller center periodically, especially in categories that have seen recent enforcement activity — enforcement waves are visible in seller communities before they reach your account.

Audit your active listings quarterly. Look for description language, photos, or settings that may have fallen out of compliance as requirements evolved. A listing that was fine when created can become a violation months later without anyone touching it.

Most sellers who run into policy problems weren't trying to cheat the system. They listed something they shouldn't have without checking, used a photo they found online not realizing it was copyrighted, or kept doing something the old way after the rules changed. The violations that are genuinely avoidable aren't the clever schemes — they're the oversights. Pay attention, stay current, and treat compliance as maintenance rather than bureaucracy.

Chapter 23: Account Suspension Prevention

Account suspension represents the nuclear option in eBay's enforcement arsenal, capable of destroying years of business building overnight while leaving sellers with limited recourse and mountains of stranded inventory. The platform's automated enforcement systems operate with the subtlety of a sledgehammer, often suspending accounts first and investigating later, if at all.

The best suspension prevention strategy is boring: keep your metrics clean, your listings accurate, and your policies current. Account health rarely fails catastrophically from a single event — it deteriorates through accumulated small problems that compound until the algorithm decides the account is more trouble than it's worth. This chapter covers both the prevention habits and what to do when enforcement happens anyway.

Understanding eBay's Enforcement Mechanisms

eBay's enforcement is automated first, human second — and the human review, when it happens, usually upholds the algorithmic decision. Accounts get flagged by software, suspended by software, and appealed to people who are working from the same information the algorithm used. The seller's perspective is often the last thing considered, if it's considered at all.

The algorithm is watching your defect rate, your late shipment rate, your response time, your return rate, and how your buyers rate you. It's also watching for patterns that suggest policy violations — related accounts, prohibited item keywords, rapid listing volume changes. Most of what triggers enforcement action is measurable and visible in your seller dashboard if you know where to look.

Machine learning enforcement catches violations it was trained to catch and occasionally triggers on things it wasn't. Sellers who list large quantities of the same item in a new category can trip fraud filters. Sellers who list items with keywords that appear in prohibited listings can get flagged even when their items are completely legitimate. These are frustrating false positives and they happen.

When a human reviewer looks at a case, they're typically working through a queue with limited time. They see what the algorithm flagged and whatever the seller submitted in response. A well-documented appeal with specific factual rebuttals to the alleged violation stands a better chance than an emotional narrative about how long you've been selling on eBay.

Enforcement typically escalates through warning, listing removal, selling restriction, fee hold, and then suspension. Each step gives you an opportunity to correct course before the next one. Sellers who respond to warnings seriously — not defensively — usually avoid suspension. Sellers who ignore warnings or argue instead of fixing things tend to keep escalating until the account is gone.

The appeals process exists, but win rates are low. eBay's default position in appeals is that the initial decision was correct. Overturning it requires specific, documented evidence that the decision was wrong — not that you're a good seller, not that you've been on eBay for fifteen years, not that you don't understand why this happened. Evidence that the specific alleged violation didn't occur, or that the metrics the suspension was based on were in error.

> ★ **Pro Tip:** Monitor your seller dashboard daily for any warnings, policy notifications, or metric changes that could signal developing enforcement issues before they escalate to account restrictions.

Seller Performance Metrics Management

Your seller metrics aren't just numbers on a dashboard — they're eBay's primary tool for deciding whether you're running a business they want on their platform. Poor metrics trigger algorithmic action even without a specific policy violation. This means a supplier who ships slow, a product with a high return rate, or a habit of uploading tracking late can damage your account regardless of how well you handle everything else.

The defect rate counts cases closed without seller resolution, item not received claims, and significantly not as described cases as a percentage of transactions. Keep it below 2%. Above that threshold, eBay starts restricting your account. The metric resets on a rolling basis, so a bad month doesn't permanently damage you — but it also means you can't coast on past performance.

Late shipment rate is exactly what it sounds like — the percentage of items shipped after your stated handling time. Keep it below 3%. The most common cause isn't actually late shipping — it's late tracking uploads. Carriers scan packages late or not at all, and eBay counts that against you. Upload tracking immediately when you create the label, not when you actually drop off the package.

High return rates in specific categories or on specific products usually mean one of two things: the listing isn't accurate, or the product isn't good. Both are fixable. An item with a 10% return rate is sending a clear signal that something in the description or photos doesn't match what buyers receive. Find the gap and close it.

Response time matters for your metrics and for buyers. eBay tracks how quickly you respond to messages and factors it into your seller standing. The sellers who struggle most with response time are the ones who let weekends and evenings go unchecked. Even a brief reply that says "I'll have more information for you tomorrow" counts as a timely response and keeps the clock from running against you.

Upload tracking within the handling time you promised — not when you get around to it. This is a metric eBay measures precisely and penalizes consistently. Buyers who see tracking uploaded immediately after purchase have lower anxiety. eBay has better data for its metrics. Everyone benefits from this habit being automatic rather than occasional.

eBay Rewards System Progression

eBay's seller rewards system creates incentives for consistent performance through Top Rated Seller and Power Seller programs that offer fee discounts and enhanced visibility for sellers who maintain excellent metrics. Top Rated Seller status requires meeting performance standards for shipping time, tracking uploads, and customer service metrics that demonstrate professional operations.

Power Seller levels (Bronze through Titanium) depend on sales volume and account standing, providing increasing benefits as business grows. These programs reward sellers who follow eBay policies consistently while providing excellent customer service that maintains high feedback scores. The progression system encourages professional behavior while providing tangible benefits that improve profitability for sellers who invest in quality operations instead of cutting corners that damage long-term account health.

Proactive Compliance Monitoring

The most effective compliance monitoring is boring and routine: check your seller dashboard weekly, read policy update emails instead of deleting them, and review active listings periodically to confirm they still comply with current requirements. eBay changes policies without sending individual notices to every seller. What was acceptable last year may not be acceptable now, and the seller who finds out from an enforcement action is always behind.

Go through your active listings quarterly at minimum. Look for description language that doesn't match current eBay category standards, photos that no longer represent the actual item if anything has changed, and pricing or shipping settings that might have drifted out of compliance. A listing that was fine when created can become a problem as eBay's category requirements evolve.

eBay publishes policy updates in its seller announcements and help center. Make reading those a monthly habit. When a policy changes in your category, assume it applies to your existing listings immediately — because it does. The "I didn't know the policy changed" appeal doesn't carry much weight.

Pay attention to enforcement trends in your category. Seller forums and communities discuss enforcement patterns, and patterns repeat. A category that sees a wave of listing removals or account restrictions is showing you where eBay's current attention is focused. Get ahead of it rather than waiting to see if you're next.

Keep records that pre-date any enforcement action. Transaction history, supplier correspondence, photos taken before shipping — this documentation is what you need when you have to demonstrate that your business operates legitimately. After an enforcement action happens is too late to start gathering it.

If you operate in a regulated category — health products, electronics with safety certifications, items with age restrictions — professional compliance review is worth the cost at the revenue level where your account matters to your livelihood. The specifics of what eBay requires in those categories change and aren't always clearly documented in the general policy pages.

▲ **Caution:** Don't assume that practices which worked previously will remain compliant. eBay policy interpretations and enforcement priorities change regularly without grandfathering existing operations.

Risk Factor Identification and Mitigation

Some seller situations carry higher inherent risk. Knowing which ones helps you manage accordingly rather than being surprised when enforcement attention shows up.

High-risk categories — supplements, electronics, children's items, replica-adjacent products — face heavier enforcement attention because buyer complaint rates are higher there. If you sell in these categories, your metrics and your listing accuracy need to be cleaner than average, not the same as average. The margin for error is smaller.

Rapid growth trips fraud detection algorithms. A seller who goes from twenty listings to two thousand in a month, or who suddenly starts doing ten times their usual transaction volume, looks like either a compromised account or an operation that scaled past legitimate sourcing. Scale gradually and document your sourcing as you grow.

International selling creates compliance complexity. Customs delays generate "item not received" claims. Language barriers create communication gaps that turn into disputes. Shipping to certain countries creates return logistics problems. Know which markets actually work for your business model before expanding into them rather than discovering the problems after the metrics are already damaged.

New accounts are under more scrutiny than established ones. eBay's algorithm doesn't trust accounts without history, and enforcement thresholds are lower. Build volume slowly, keep metrics perfect in the early months, and don't list anything borderline until your account has enough positive history to absorb a mistake.

Multiple accounts are a serious risk. eBay prohibits operating multiple seller accounts without explicit permission, and its detection systems look for related accounts through shared IP addresses, bank accounts, payment methods, and device fingerprints. If a family member sells on eBay from your household or your business address, that connection is discoverable and can create account linkage violations that weren't intentional but still result in suspension.

Your suppliers' behavior affects your account. A dropshipping supplier who ships retail-packaged products directly to buyers, whose items frequently generate complaints, or whose shipping times consistently miss your stated windows is a liability. You're responsible for your metrics regardless of where the problem originated.

Account Health Maintenance Strategies

Account health is just good operations practiced consistently. There's no trick to it. Accurate listings reduce returns. Fast shipping improves metrics. Responsive customer service prevents cases. The sellers with healthy accounts aren't doing anything exotic — they're doing the fundamentals well every day without letting standards slip when things get busy.

Resolve buyer problems before they become cases. A case that gets closed in your favor still counts differently in your metrics than one that never opened. The path that protects your account best is usually the one that resolves the buyer's concern before they click the dispute button.

Inspect items before listing and before shipping. Items that don't match their description generate returns and defects. The two-minute inspection before shipping that catches a condition problem is worth much more than the hour of customer service the problem would create if it ships anyway.

Keep your communication through eBay's messaging system. It's documented, timestamped, and available to eBay if a dispute goes to review. Off-platform communication — even when the buyer initiates it — isn't visible to eBay and can't be submitted as evidence in a dispute. Follow up any off-platform conversation with a message through the eBay system summarizing what was discussed.

Ship within your stated handling time. This sounds obvious but it's the single metric that trips up the most sellers during busy periods. When order volume increases, handling time pressure goes up proportionally. Either set a longer handling time that you can actually meet during peak periods, or scale your shipping operations to match the volume. Don't set optimistic handling times that only work when you're not busy.

Handle returns efficiently. Slow, disputed return processing is a metric problem. Even returns that feel unfair are better processed quickly and cleanly. A return that finishes in two days causes less metric damage than one that drags for two weeks while you argue about it.

Keep financial reserves. eBay can hold funds during enforcement actions or when your account is under review. Sellers who depend on immediate access to every dollar in their eBay account for operating expenses discover this problem at the worst possible time. Have enough cushion that a hold doesn't stop you from shipping orders or paying suppliers.

> ■ **Danger Zone:** Never ignore early warning signs like policy notifications, metric declines, or buyer complaints. Small problems compound quickly and can trigger enforcement actions that destroy entire businesses.

Crisis Response and Damage Control

When you get an enforcement notice, read it carefully before responding. Understand specifically what eBay alleges you did wrong. Many sellers respond emotionally to the fact of enforcement rather than the substance of it — and that's why their appeals fail. You can't rebut something you haven't read carefully.

Gather your documentation immediately. Transaction records, communication logs, photos taken before shipping, supplier agreements — whatever is relevant to the specific violation alleged. Do this before you appeal, not during. An appeal submitted with complete documentation is treated differently from one that promises to send documentation later.

Write your appeal factually, not emotionally. Address the specific allegation with specific evidence. Don't explain how many years you've been on eBay or how many positive feedbacks you have — those things don't override the specific violation eBay identified. Show why the specific thing they say you did either didn't happen or doesn't constitute a violation under the policy they cited.

While the appeal is in process, don't stop selling on other platforms. eBay's appeal process can take weeks. If your only revenue is eBay and it's frozen while you appeal, the pressure that creates will push you into making reactive decisions. Have other options active so you can wait out the process calmly.

For serious enforcement actions involving significant account value or business income, professional representation is worth considering. There are consultants who specialize in eBay reinstatement and understand what specific appeals need to include to succeed. The cost of that expertise is often less than the cost of failing the appeal.

Notify suppliers and other business contacts about the situation before it affects them. If you have pending orders, active supplier agreements, or obligations that will be disrupted by a suspension, communicating early gives those relationships a chance to adapt rather than discovering the problem when an order doesn't ship.

Long-term Account Protection Strategies

The most effective long-term protection against suspension is not building your entire livelihood around a single platform. eBay can suspend an account, freeze funds, or change policies in ways that directly harm your business, and there's no due process that guarantees a fair outcome. Sellers who depend entirely on eBay income are one enforcement action away from serious financial disruption.

Sell on multiple platforms. eBay is valuable, but Amazon, Etsy, your own website, or other marketplaces that fit your product mix provide income continuity when eBay has problems. Platform diversification is business risk management, not disloyalty to eBay.

Stay current with policy changes as a regular business habit. eBay's policies change more frequently than most sellers realize, and the updates aren't always announced prominently. Sellers who stay current through eBay's seller announcements, community forums, and industry news tend to adapt before enforcement happens rather than after.

Use automation for compliance monitoring at scale. At high listing volume, manual review of every listing for ongoing compliance isn't realistic. Tools that flag keyword issues, category mismatches, or performance metric changes let you catch problems early without requiring you to personally review everything.

Keep financial reserves outside of eBay. Funds held in your eBay account are accessible to eBay. During an enforcement action, those funds can be held or offset against alleged liabilities. Your operating capital and reserves should be in accounts that eBay doesn't control.

If your business depends on eBay revenue at a level that would materially affect your finances if the account was suspended, know an e-commerce attorney before you need one. Establishing that relationship when things are going well is much easier than finding competent representation in a crisis.

The central reality of eBay account protection is that prevention is the only strategy that reliably works. Reinstatement after suspension is difficult, slow, and uncertain. Appeals succeed less often than sellers expect. The time and energy spent fighting enforcement actions is time not spent growing the business. Build the habits that make enforcement unlikely, and the account health tends to take care of itself.

Chapter 24: Legal and Tax Considerations

Legal and tax obligations for eBay sellers have transformed from simple hobby reporting requirements into complex compliance challenges that can trigger audits, penalties, and legal liability when ignored or mishandled. The days of treating eBay sales as casual income that doesn't warrant professional attention disappeared when governments discovered the revenue potential of taxing online commerce.

Most eBay sellers discover the legal and tax side of their business the expensive way — through a surprise tax bill, a liability they didn't see coming, or a compliance requirement they ignored too long. This chapter covers what actually matters for eBay sellers, in plain terms, without the bureaucratic framing that makes most legal and tax writing unreadable.

Business Structure and Entity Formation

Choosing a business structure is a real decision with lasting consequences, and most eBay sellers either never make it deliberately or default to sole proprietorship without understanding what that means. The short version: as a sole proprietor, your business and your personal finances are legally the same thing. If someone sues over a product you sold, your personal assets are on the table. That's fine when you're selling a few hundred dollars a year. It's a meaningful risk when your eBay income is substantial and you're selling products that carry any liability exposure.

An LLC is the most practical structure for most serious eBay sellers. It puts a legal wall between the business and your personal assets, which can matter a great deal if something goes wrong. It's not complicated to set up — most states have an online filing process — and it doesn't change how you pay taxes much. You file a Schedule C either way until you elect otherwise. The cost is a filing fee and usually a small annual fee to maintain the registration.

Corporations offer stronger liability protection but add real complexity — separate tax filings, more formalities, payroll considerations if you want the tax advantages. For most solo eBay sellers, the LLC does everything the business needs without that overhead. If your situation is unusual or your business is growing toward significant scale, talk to a business attorney rather than relying on general guidance.

> ★ **Pro Tip:** Consult with a business attorney and tax professional before choosing business structure. The right choice depends on your specific situation and long-term business goals.

If you sell with a partner — a spouse, a friend, a business associate — you need a formal agreement regardless of how much you trust each other. What happens to the business if one person wants out? Who gets what share of the profits? Who decides what to sell? These questions are easy to answer when the relationship is good and hard to answer when it isn't. A simple operating agreement that addresses these things costs a few hundred dollars with an attorney and prevents the kind of disputes that destroy both businesses and relationships.

Business licensing is the piece most eBay sellers ignore until it becomes a problem. Many states and localities require a reseller's permit or general business license once you're operating with any regularity. A reseller's permit also allows you to buy inventory wholesale without paying sales tax — which matters if your sourcing involves any wholesale suppliers. Check your state's requirements rather than assuming casual selling exempts you. The threshold for "running a business" is lower than most people think.

Sales Tax Collection and Remittance

The good news on sales tax is that eBay handles most of it for you. Following the 2018 Wayfair Supreme Court decision, eBay automatically collects and remits sales tax on your behalf in states that require it. You don't register, file, or remit anything for those states — eBay does it. That's a significant administrative burden that used to fall entirely on sellers and now doesn't.

What eBay doesn't handle is your income tax. The platform reports your sales to the IRS once you exceed certain thresholds — currently $600 in a calendar year under the updated 1099-K rules, though this threshold has shifted and may shift again. Check current IRS guidance rather than relying on what applied in previous years. The sale proceeds are income regardless of whether you receive a 1099.

If you sell to tax-exempt buyers — businesses purchasing for resale, nonprofits — they may request that you not charge sales tax on transactions. eBay's platform handles tax-exempt purchases through their own system; you don't typically need to manage exemption certificates manually for eBay sales. If you sell through channels outside eBay, that's a different situation worth discussing with a tax professional.

Income Tax Reporting and Business Deductions

eBay is not a hobby. The IRS doesn't care that you started selling to clear out your garage. If you're doing this with any regularity and intent to make money, it's business income. That means all of it counts — sale proceeds, shipping charges you collect, everything — whether or not eBay or PayPal sends you a 1099. Get a tax professional who understands e-commerce before your first tax year, not after it.

The good news is that legitimate business expenses reduce your taxable income dollar for dollar. Inventory costs, shipping supplies, packaging, storage, mileage driving to thrift stores and post offices, subscriptions to listing tools — these all count. The key is keeping records as you go rather than reconstructing everything in April from memory and bank statements.

Home office deductions are real but specific. The space has to be used exclusively and regularly for business — a dedicated corner of a room where you photograph, pack, and manage eBay operations. It can't also be the guest bedroom. If it qualifies, you deduct the percentage of your home's square footage that the space represents against rent or mortgage interest, utilities, and insurance.

Equipment — cameras, computers, printers, scales — depreciates over time for tax purposes, though Section 179 often lets you deduct the full cost in the year of purchase for smaller businesses. Your accountant can tell you which approach makes more sense for your situation in a given year. Don't guess; the rules have nuances that shift with tax law changes.

Inventory accounting is where most eBay sellers get sloppy. You need to know what you paid for every item you sell — that's your cost of goods sold, which reduces your taxable profit. The method you choose (FIFO, specific identification, weighted average) affects your tax liability and needs to be consistent year to year. For most eBay sellers tracking individual items, specific identification is the most defensible approach.

Self-employment tax is the one that surprises new sellers. Beyond income tax, you owe 15.3% self-employment tax on net profit from the business. That's the employer and employee portions of Social Security and Medicare that a regular job would split. Factor this into your pricing from the start — sellers who ignore it discover it when they owe a large unexpected amount at filing.

> ▲ **Caution:** Maintain detailed records of all business income and expenses. The IRS expects professional record keeping standards regardless of your business size or sophistication level.

Product Liability and Insurance Considerations

Liability follows the seller. If a product you sold injures someone, the legal claim is against you — not the manufacturer, not the supplier, not eBay. The manufacturer may be overseas and unreachable. The supplier may have disappeared. You're the one with a US address who took payment. General liability insurance provides protection; personal homeowner's or renter's policies explicitly exclude business activities and won't cover you.

Some products require specific safety notices, age restriction language, or usage warnings as a condition of legal sale. Children's products, certain electronics, chemical products, and food-adjacent items have specific labeling requirements. Selling something without required labels doesn't just create legal exposure — it can result in mandatory recall participation and buyer notification obligations that are expensive and time-consuming.

Product recalls create obligations even after the sale. If a manufacturer recalls something you sold, you may need to notify buyers and participate in the recall process. The Consumer Product Safety Commission database is publicly searchable — check it periodically against your inventory categories, especially for electronics and children's items.

Professional liability coverage protects against claims related to business advice, consultation, or professional services that some eBay sellers provide alongside their product sales.

> ■ **Danger Zone:** Never assume your homeowner's or renter's insurance covers business activities. Most personal policies exclude commercial activities and provide no protection for eBay selling liability.

Import/Export Regulations and Customs Compliance

International selling adds customs complexity most eBay sellers underestimate until something goes wrong. Declare accurately — product value, country of origin, content description. Don't let buyers pressure you into undervaluing shipments to reduce their import duties. Customs fraud is a real offense and the obligation is yours, not the buyer's.

What's legal to sell domestically isn't necessarily legal to ship internationally. Certain knives, electronics with specific radio frequencies, weapons accessories, health supplements, and items made from protected materials are prohibited in various destination countries. Research restrictions before shipping to new markets, not after a package is seized.

Intellectual Property Protection and Infringement Risks

IP enforcement on eBay is active. Major brands run automated monitoring that flags listings containing their trademarks or images. A complaint from a rights holder can remove your listing and potentially trigger account action. The rules are worth understanding because the most common violations are also the most avoidable.

Selling genuine branded products is legal under first sale doctrine — you bought it, you can resell it. Where it gets complicated: using brand names in your title when the item isn't that brand, bundling branded products in ways that modify original packaging, or implying manufacturer authorization that doesn't exist.

Take your own photos. Using manufacturer images without permission is copyright infringement regardless of how common the practice is. Rights holders do send DMCA takedowns, and repeated violations create liability beyond listing removal.

Counterfeit goods carry criminal liability, not just account penalties. "I didn't know" is not a complete defense. If a supplier's prices seem implausibly low for branded goods, that's your signal. Don't assume legitimacy — verify it.

Record Keeping and Documentation Requirements

Keep everything, organize it as you go, don't rely on reconstruction later. The sellers who struggle at tax time are almost always the ones who kept records intermittently. The ones who sail through built habits that captured information in real time.

For every sale: what you sold, what you paid for it, what shipping cost, the final price, the date. eBay's transaction reports give you most of this, but you need to add your cost basis for each item — eBay doesn't know what you paid at the estate sale. That cost basis is your cost of goods sold, which reduces your taxable profit.

Keep a separate business checking account and business credit card. When business income and expenses run through the same accounts as personal finances, every tax question requires untangling the two. Separate accounts make the business transparent and record-keeping significantly easier.

Save everything compliance-related: your reseller's permit, business license, any exemption certificates from wholesale customers, your insurance policy, and professional agreements. These documents prove your business operates legitimately if anyone asks.

eBay messaging history is business communication. Screenshot significant buyer interactions — disputes, complaints, anything that resulted in a refund or exception. These records support your position if a dispute escalates or eBay questions a transaction months later when your memory has faded.

The IRS expects you to keep tax records for at least three years from the filing date. The practical approach: keep everything for seven years. Storage is cheap, audits are rare, and the records you don't have are always the ones that matter most when they happen.

Legal and tax compliance won't make you money directly — but ignoring it can cost far more than the professional guidance required to get it right. An accountant who knows e-commerce pays for themselves in the deductions they find and the problems they prevent. Get one before your first real tax year, not after the expensive mistakes.

PART VI: Scaling and Optimization

Chapter 25: Automation Tools and Software

Automation tools for eBay selling promise to transform your manual labor into effortless profits while you sip cocktails on beaches and watch money flow into your bank account. The reality involves expensive software subscriptions, complex integrations, and automated systems that often create more problems than they solve when they malfunction at the worst possible moments.

The sellers who get real value from automation are the ones who identify the specific tasks eating their time and find tools that handle those tasks reliably. The ones who don't get value are the ones who bought subscriptions hoping automation would fix problems that were actually sourcing problems, listing problems, or pricing problems. Automation doesn't fix those. It just runs them faster.

Listing Management and Creation Software

Listing automation software helps manage large inventories by simplifying the creation, modification, and optimization of eBay listings through templates, bulk editing capabilities, and automated posting schedules that reduce manual work.

Template systems allow creating listing frameworks that maintain consistent formatting, policy information, and presentation standards across hundreds or thousands of items while enabling customization for specific products and categories.

Bulk listing tools process multiple items simultaneously through CSV uploads, database imports, or API integrations that dramatically reduce the time required to create large numbers of listings compared to manual entry.

Listing optimization features analyze performance data to suggest title improvements, category adjustments, and pricing modifications that enhance search visibility and conversion rates based on historical sales patterns.

> ★ **Pro Tip:** Start with basic automation features and gradually add complexity as you master each tool. Rushing into advanced automation often creates operational disasters that consume more time than manual processes.

Scheduled posting capabilities distribute listing launches across optimal timing windows to maximize exposure while avoiding overwhelming buyers with simultaneous inventory dumps that dilute individual item visibility.

Cross-platform integration enables managing eBay listings alongside Amazon, Facebook Marketplace, and other selling channels through unified interfaces that prevent overselling and maintain inventory accuracy.

Inventory Synchronization and Management Systems

Inventory management automation prevents overselling, tracks costs, and maintains accurate stock levels across multiple selling platforms while providing analytics that guide purchasing and pricing decisions.

Real-time inventory tracking monitors stock levels continuously and automatically adjusts or removes listings when items become unavailable, preventing overselling situations that create customer service disasters and policy violations.

Cost basis tracking maintains detailed records of inventory acquisition costs, fees, and associated expenses that enable accurate profitability analysis and tax reporting for business operations.

Supplier integration connects with wholesale partners and dropshipping sources to automatically update product information, pricing changes, and availability status without manual monitoring and adjustment.

Warehouse management features help organize physical inventory through location tracking, barcode systems, and pick lists that simplify fulfillment operations for sellers managing significant inventory volumes.

Low stock alerts notify sellers when inventory levels approach reorder points, enabling proactive purchasing decisions that prevent stockouts during peak selling periods.

Seasonal adjustment tools modify inventory strategies based on historical demand patterns, automatically adjusting pricing and promotion schedules to optimize sales during different market conditions.

Order Processing and Fulfillment Automation

Order automation simplifies fulfillment workflows from payment confirmation through delivery tracking while maintaining customer communication standards that support buyer satisfaction and seller metrics.

Payment verification systems automatically confirm transaction completion and trigger fulfillment processes without manual intervention, reducing processing delays that affect shipping performance metrics.

Shipping label generation integrates with carrier systems to automatically create shipping labels, calculate postage, and select optimal shipping methods based on package dimensions, destination, and cost parameters.

Tracking upload automation submits tracking information to eBay immediately when labels are created, improving seller metrics while providing buyers with shipment visibility that reduces customer service inquiries.

▲ **Caution:** Over-automation can create customer service problems when buyers need personal attention that automated systems cannot provide. Maintain human oversight for complex situations.

Customer communication workflows send automated order confirmations, shipping notifications, and delivery updates that maintain professional communication standards while reducing manual messaging requirements.

Exception handling systems identify orders that require special attention due to address issues, payment problems, or unusual circumstances that demand manual review before automated processing.

Return processing automation manages return authorizations, shipping labels, and inventory restoration while maintaining compliance with eBay policies and customer service standards.

Repricing and Competitive Analysis Tools

Automated repricing tools monitor competitor pricing and market conditions to adjust your prices dynamically while protecting profit margins and maintaining competitive positioning in rapidly changing markets.

Repricing tools earn their subscription cost quickly if you're selling in competitive categories. Without one, staying priced correctly across hundreds of listings means either checking manually every day — which nobody actually does consistently — or accepting that you're regularly priced too high to sell or too low to profit.

Good repricing tools watch what competitors are doing — when they drop prices, when they sell out, when new sellers enter your category. That intelligence is available without the tools, but synthesizing it across a large inventory manually isn't realistic.

The key setting in any repricing system is your price floor. Set it carefully — accounting for all fees, shipping, and a real profit margin — and let the tool work within that boundary. Repricing tools that don't respect a hard floor will race you to the bottom against other automated sellers until nobody is making money.

Use repricing data to spot market shifts, not just react to them. If your tool keeps hitting the floor in a category without generating sales, that's a signal that demand has dropped or the market is oversupplied — a sourcing problem, not a pricing problem.

Customer Service and Communication Automation

The communication side of eBay scales badly without some automation. At twenty sales a month, you can write every message personally. At two hundred, you can't — not without it consuming your evenings. Saved templates for the messages you send repeatedly are the minimum viable solution. They're not glamorous, but they work.

Write templates that sound like you wrote them fresh. "Your order shipped today — tracking number above. Let me know if anything looks off when it arrives." That takes five seconds to personalize and feels personal. A template that reads like an autoresponder from 2009 does not.

Automated order confirmations and shipping notifications handle the routine touchpoints. The human attention should go to anything that doesn't fit the template — questions that suggest a buyer is uncertain, messages with any tone of frustration, return requests. Those conversations need a real person, not a canned response.

Watch your response time metrics. eBay tracks how fast you reply and factors it into your seller standing. Most sellers do fine during the week but let messages sit over weekends. That pattern alone can pull down metrics that take months to rebuild.

If you sell internationally, translation tools reduce friction with overseas buyers significantly. Basic automated translations for standard messages handle most situations. For anything complex or dispute-adjacent, take the extra few minutes to make sure the translation actually says what you intend.

> ■ **Danger Zone:** Never rely entirely on automated customer service. Human judgment remains essential for complex situations, dispute resolution, and maintaining buyer relationships.

Analytics and Performance Monitoring Software

Most sellers know roughly how much they're making. Far fewer know which specific items and categories are actually generating that profit versus which ones are dragging the average down. Analytics tools answer that question, and the answer is usually surprising. The items you think are your workhorses sometimes aren't.

Track revenue and profit separately. Revenue is flattering. Profit is what actually matters. A tool that shows you gross sales without accounting for eBay fees, shipping costs, and cost of goods is showing you a number that feels good and means nothing. You need to see what's left after everything comes out.

Pay attention to traffic versus conversion separately. An item getting views but no sales has a price or presentation problem. An item getting no views has a title or category problem. These are different diagnoses that need different fixes, and lumping them together as "not selling" wastes time on the wrong solution.

Seasonal patterns in your own sales data are more valuable than generic seasonal advice. Your specific categories, your specific customer base, your specific price points may behave differently from the averages. Run your own numbers over twelve months before you trust anyone's general guidance about when to source or when to discount.

Whatever analytics platform you use, make sure it exports data in a format your accountant can work with. The reporting that looks great inside a selling tool sometimes requires significant cleanup before it's useful for taxes. Find that out before January, not during it.

Integration Platforms and API Management

At a certain scale, your eBay tools need to talk to each other. A repricing tool that doesn't know your inventory levels will keep adjusting prices on items you can't fulfill. An order management system that doesn't sync with your shipping carrier will require manual label entry on every order. The point of integration platforms is to eliminate these gaps — connecting your eBay account, inventory tracking, shipping, accounting, and communication tools into a single workflow that updates automatically as things happen.

Most of this happens through APIs — the connections that let different software systems exchange data in real time. You don't need to understand how APIs work technically, but you do need to know whether your tools support them. A tool that can't connect to anything else creates a data island you'll have to update manually, which defeats the purpose of having the tool.

Two things matter that sellers usually skip: backups and access control. Your business data — listings, customer records, pricing history, supplier contacts — has real value and is genuinely at risk from software failures, account compromises, or just a tool shutting down unexpectedly. Back it up regularly to something you control. And limit what each tool can access. A repricing tool doesn't need access to your financial records. A VA doesn't need admin credentials to your main account. Keep access scoped to what each system actually requires.

Cost-Benefit Analysis and ROI Evaluation

Before subscribing to any automation tool, run the actual math on what it costs. The monthly fee is the obvious number, but it's not the whole picture. Add your time for setup, for learning the tool, for maintaining it when things break, and for reviewing its output to catch errors. A $30/month tool that takes two hours a week to manage properly costs you more than $30/month.

The return side of the calculation needs to be equally specific. Not "this saves me time" but "this specific task took me X hours a week and now takes Y." Not "this improves accuracy" but "before this tool I had Z errors a month that each cost me W minutes to fix." Vague ROI claims justify buying tools you don't need. Specific numbers tell you whether a tool earns its place.

Automation earns its cost when it frees you to do things the business needs that only you can do — better sourcing, stronger supplier relationships, smarter pricing decisions. It doesn't earn its cost when it just adds subscription fees to operations that were already working fine. Evaluate each tool on that basis and you'll make better decisions about what to adopt and what to skip.

Chapter 26: Building Multiple Revenue Streams

The longer you sell exclusively on eBay, the more vulnerable you become to things outside your control. Policy changes, algorithm shifts, enforcement actions, fee increases — any of these can cut your revenue significantly overnight. Building other income sources isn't just growth strategy. It's what separates sellers who survive bad eBay years from those who don't.

The good news is that the skills you've built on eBay — sourcing, photographing, describing, shipping, customer service — transfer directly to other selling contexts. You're not starting over on a new platform. You're deploying what you already know in a different environment.

Expanding to Additional Selling Platforms

Adding platforms is the most direct way to protect against eBay dependence, and your existing inventory is already there. The same item sitting in your storage room can be listed on Amazon, Facebook Marketplace, Mercari, and Etsy simultaneously. The challenge isn't the inventory — it's learning each platform's specific rules, buyer expectations, and fee structures well enough to price correctly and avoid problems.

Amazon is the obvious first expansion for most eBay sellers, and the most demanding. The fee structure is different, the listing requirements are strict, and the competition is intense. Amazon's buyers expect Prime-level service regardless of whether you're a huge operation or a solo seller. The traffic is massive and the customers are ready to buy — but the margin pressure is real and the learning curve is steeper than most sellers expect.

Facebook Marketplace is underrated by sellers who associate it with people selling used furniture. It works well for local pickup items, larger pieces, and anything where buyers want to inspect in person before buying. No shipping means no shipping costs or claims. The audience is local and transaction volume is lower, but it's a clean, low-friction channel for the right inventory.

Mercari has grown significantly and handles a wide range of categories with a mobile-first buyer base. The fees are competitive, listing is fast, and buyers are generally reasonable. It doesn't have eBay's depth in collectibles or specialty categories, but for general merchandise it's worth a look.

Poshmark is fashion-focused and community-driven. It rewards sellers who engage with the platform actively — sharing listings, following others, participating in posh parties. If your inventory doesn't include clothing, shoes, or accessories, it's not the right fit. If it does, the buyer base is loyal and willing to pay fair prices for quality items.

Etsy works best for vintage items, handmade goods, and craft supplies. If you source estate sale items with genuine age or sell anything with a handmade element, Etsy buyers are often willing to pay more than eBay buyers for the same item because the platform positions things as special rather than commodity.

Once you're on more than one platform, inventory synchronization becomes critical. An item that sells on eBay needs to come down on Mercari immediately. Manual management works at low volume; at any meaningful scale you need software that talks to all your platforms simultaneously.

> ★ **Pro Tip:** Start with one additional platform and master its requirements before expanding further. Each platform has unique rules and customer expectations that require focused attention to implement successfully.

Developing Private Label Products

Private label is the path from reseller to brand owner. Instead of finding someone else's product and selling it alongside everyone else who found the same product, you source your own version — with your branding, your specifications, your packaging — and sell something competitors can't simply copy-list beneath you. It's more work and more upfront investment than reselling, but the margins and the moat are both significantly better.

Start with products where you have real knowledge. If you've been reselling vintage audio equipment for years, you understand what buyers in that market care about — what features matter, what quality means to them, what price points work. That knowledge is what lets you identify where an existing product falls short and where a private label version could win.

The supplier relationship for private label is different from dropshipping. You're specifying the product, not just ordering from a catalog. That means minimum order quantities, samples, feedback rounds, and potentially longer lead times. It also means you own the product once it exists — the manufacturer can't sell your exact version to your competitors.

Brand development doesn't require expensive agencies or elaborate identities. A clean logo, consistent packaging, and a name that buyers can remember are enough to start. What makes a private label brand work is product quality and customer experience, not design sophistication. Buyers who receive something that works well and looks professional will come back regardless of whether the branding is elaborate.

Quality control is where private label either works or doesn't. The manufacturer will maintain whatever standard you specify — or slightly below it, over time, if you're not paying attention. Inspect samples regularly. Visit the factory if the volume justifies it. Use a third-party inspection service if you can't be there yourself. Your brand is only as good as what arrives in buyers' hands.

Register your trademark before you need to. Trademark registration in the US is straightforward and relatively inexpensive. Discovering that someone has registered your brand name after you've spent a year building it — or that a competitor has filed a complaint against you using their own trademark — is the expensive version of this lesson.

Marketing a private label product requires more effort than listing a resale item because you're creating awareness from scratch. eBay SEO, promoted listings, product reviews, and eventually off-platform channels all contribute. Build in patience — private label brands take months to gain traction, not weeks.

Wholesale and B2B Opportunities

If you've developed genuine expertise in a product category — you know the right suppliers, you understand what quality looks like, you can evaluate inventory quickly — other sellers will pay for access to that knowledge. Wholesale means becoming the supplier instead of being the customer.

Your wholesale customers are the people who would otherwise be your competition — other online sellers, small retailers, specialty stores. They want reliable inventory at reasonable prices from someone who knows what they're selling. You're offering all three, plus the relationships you've already built with manufacturers or distributors who aren't easy to reach.

Wholesale pricing needs to work for both parties. You need enough margin to justify selling at lower-than-retail prices. Your customer needs enough margin to sell at retail and make a profit. That math works differently at different volume levels — figure out your floor price at different quantities and be clear about it upfront rather than negotiating on every order.

Payment terms are a significant shift from retail. Net 30 is standard in wholesale — you ship, they pay 30 days later. That requires carrying the receivable, which requires cash. Don't extend terms to customers until you've verified they're creditworthy, and start new relationships with smaller orders on prepayment terms before extending credit.

Exclusive territory agreements can build stronger relationships with high-volume customers, but commit to them cautiously. Locking yourself out of competing markets in exchange for volume promises that don't materialize is a common wholesale mistake. Earn the exclusivity conversation by proving volume first.

Trade shows — both as an exhibitor and as an attendee — are worth considering once your wholesale operation reaches a certain scale. The relationships built in person convert faster than email relationships, and seeing what buyers and competitors are doing in your category in one room is a useful market research exercise you can't replicate online.

> ▲ **Caution:** Wholesale relationships require different customer service standards and business practices than retail selling. Understand the commitment before pursuing wholesale opportunities.

Service-Based Revenue Streams

After enough years of eBay selling, you know things other sellers don't. How to photograph items that actually sell. How to write titles the algorithm surfaces. How to price competitively without destroying margin. How to handle the specific problems that come up in certain categories. That knowledge has value beyond your own listings.

eBay consulting is a real market. Sellers who are struggling, businesses that want to start selling online, estate sale companies looking to move inventory faster — they all need guidance that experienced sellers can provide. The fees are modest but the work fits naturally around your own selling schedule and doesn't require any additional inventory investment.

Sourcing services are simpler than they sound. You charge other sellers a fee to identify profitable inventory sources — estate sale leads, wholesale relationships, liquidation opportunities — that they couldn't find themselves. If you've spent years building these connections, turning them into a service is a low-overhead way to monetize them.

Listing services — photographing, writing, and posting items for other sellers — work well for people who have inventory but not time or skill. Estate executors, businesses liquidating equipment, collectors who want to sell but find the platform overwhelming. You bring the expertise; they bring the stuff. The fee structure varies but typically runs on a per-item or percentage-of-sale basis.

Full account management — handling someone else's eBay operation entirely, from listing through shipping and customer service — is more intensive but commands higher fees. It works best as a recurring arrangement with established clients rather than one-off engagements. The operational demands are real; don't take on more managed accounts than you can actually service at your quality standard.

If you have genuine expertise and enjoy teaching, courses and guides are worth considering. The eBay selling education market is saturated with bad advice from people who haven't actually built real businesses. Someone with a decade of real-world experience and honest, non-hype content can stand out in that environment.

Speaking opportunities exist in this space — reseller conferences, e-commerce events, library and community workshops — and they pay, though modestly. More valuable is the visibility they create for your other services and products. If you're building a consulting practice or a course business, speaking is marketing as much as it is revenue.

Physical Retail Integration

Physical retail as a complement to online selling makes more sense for some seller types than others. If you source from estate sales, auctions, and thrift stores anyway, having a physical outlet — a booth at an antique mall, a consignment arrangement, a recurring pop-up — gives you a liquidation channel for items that don't move online and a different buyer base that values the in-person experience.

Consignment works well if you have the time to manage other people's inventory alongside your own. You do the work — listing, selling, shipping — and take a percentage of the sale. The economics vary; 30–50% commission is typical. The appeal is that you need no capital tied up in inventory you own. The downside is that other people's items come with other people's expectations.

Antique mall booths are a low-commitment physical retail option. Monthly rent, no employees required, and buyers who are already in the mindset to buy. The booth becomes a showroom for items that benefit from in-person viewing — furniture, large collectibles, anything where photos don't fully communicate the appeal.

Pop-up sales and warehouse events are useful for moving large amounts of inventory quickly. The preparation time is real and the profit per item is lower than online, but the velocity is higher and the cash is immediate. Sellers who do seasonal clearance events find them effective for turning slow inventory back into working capital.

■ **Danger Zone:** Don't expand into physical retail without understanding the additional overhead, regulations, and time commitments that brick-and-mortar operations require.

Content Creation and Media Monetization

Content creation as a revenue stream only makes sense if you genuinely enjoy it and have something distinctive to say. The YouTube eBay selling space is crowded with people doing essentially the same "I made this much this month" content. What stands out is specific expertise, honest takes, and real experience — the things that make a seller's advice worth following rather than just watching.

YouTube is viable if your category has visual appeal and you can consistently produce content that teaches something useful. Thrift store and estate sale sourcing channels have genuine audiences. Niche category deep-dives — vintage electronics, specific collectibles, specialty tools — attract engaged viewers who become loyal followers. General eBay tips videos compete in an oversaturated space.

Podcasting and blogging build audiences more slowly than video but with less production overhead. They work best for sellers with strong opinions and the ability to write or speak clearly about what they know. Monetization through affiliate links, sponsorships, or course sales follows audience growth — it doesn't precede it.

Writing a book about what you actually know, like this one, is the most credibility-building thing you can do as an expert in any field. It takes time and doesn't generate income immediately, but it creates a permanent asset that opens doors to speaking, consulting, and media opportunities that don't otherwise exist.

Investment and Passive Income Development

At some point, the goal shifts from making more money to making the money you have work harder. eBay income is active — you stop working, it stops coming. Investment income keeps generating regardless of whether you're listing items or recovering from surgery or just taking a vacation. Building the second kind of income requires paying yourself consistently enough to actually invest rather than reinvesting everything back into inventory.

Real estate is the investment vehicle most e-commerce sellers gravitate toward, partly because it's tangible in a way stocks aren't. Rental income is genuinely passive once the property is managed. The capital requirements are higher and the liquidity is lower than financial markets, but for sellers who have built up significant cash reserves, it's worth serious consideration.

Index funds and bonds require less active management than real estate and provide liquidity you don't have with property. The long-term returns on diversified equity investments are well-documented. The main barrier for most eBay sellers isn't access — it's the discipline to invest consistently rather than using available cash to buy more inventory.

Buying existing eBay operations or complementary businesses is a faster path to scale than building from scratch. An estate sale company, a storage unit auction business, a competing reselling operation — acquiring an existing operation with established processes and customer relationships can compress years of organic growth into a single transaction. Evaluate acquisitions the same way you evaluate any investment: what does it actually earn, not what could it theoretically earn.

The common thread through every revenue diversification option is this: start with what you already know. The eBay seller who branches into Amazon does better than a complete newcomer because they understand marketplaces. The one who starts a consulting practice does better than a generic business coach because they have specific, tested experience. Use what you've built. Don't abandon it to start over.

Chapter 27: When to Expand Beyond eBay

There's no perfect moment to start expanding beyond eBay — but there are clear signals that you've waited too long. Sellers who treat eBay as the only platform because it's working aren't doing strategic planning. They're doing optimism. Platforms change. Algorithms shift. Fees increase. When those things happen to your only revenue source, you find out just how exposed single-platform dependence really is.

The question isn't whether to expand. The question is when — and what you expand into. This chapter covers both.

Recognizing Platform Dependency Risks

Think about what would happen to your income tomorrow if eBay suspended your account. Not because you did anything wrong — just an algorithmic mistake, a spurious complaint, a policy interpretation that goes the wrong way. If the answer is "I'd be in serious financial trouble," you're dangerously dependent on a platform that doesn't think of you as a partner. It thinks of you as a transaction.

Policy risk is real. The practices that work today — specific listing techniques, fee structures in your categories, access to certain product types — can change without warning. eBay has changed its policies significantly multiple times since 2003. Sellers who built businesses entirely around practices that later got restricted or banned discovered this at the worst possible moment.

Algorithm dependency is subtler but equally real. When eBay adjusts its search algorithm — and it does, regularly, and without announcement — traffic to established listings can drop overnight. Sellers who were on page one last month are on page four this month. If your entire business model requires eBay's algorithm to favor you, any change to that algorithm is an existential event.

Account suspension is the nuclear scenario, but it happens. Chapter 23 covers prevention in detail. The relevant point here is that sellers who have other platforms and other income sources absorb a suspension as a serious problem. Sellers who have only eBay absorb it as a business-ending event. The difference isn't skill or luck. It's preparation.

If eBay represents more than 70–80% of your total income, that's the trigger to start planning diversification. Not because something bad is about to happen, but because you're running a business with a single point of failure. The right time to build a backup is before you need one.

The competitive environment on eBay also continues to get harder. More professional operations, more automated sellers, more overseas competition. Each year the platform favors scale over individuality a little more. That's not a reason to leave eBay — but it is a reason not to assume what works now will keep working without limits.

> ★ **Pro Tip:** Start planning expansion when eBay represents more than 70% of your revenue. Waiting until you need alternative platforms creates pressure that leads to poor expansion decisions.

Market Saturation and Growth Limitations

At a certain point on eBay, doing more doesn't produce proportionally more results. You've optimized your listings, you're shipping fast, your metrics are excellent — and sales are flat. That plateau isn't a sign that you're doing something wrong. It's a sign that you've hit a ceiling that additional eBay effort won't raise.

Saturated categories are the most common cause. When a category has too many sellers relative to buyers, price becomes the only differentiator and margins compress to the point where the work stops being worth it. You can win on price for a while, but you can't out-compete overseas operations with no overhead indefinitely. If your category is saturated, the answer is usually to find a different category or a different platform — not to optimize harder.

Search visibility on eBay favors established sellers with strong metrics, sales history, and promotional budgets. New listings from newer sellers or in crowded categories start at a disadvantage that only promoted listings spending can partially overcome. If your organic visibility keeps declining and promoted listings are the only thing sustaining sales, your effective margin is already being eroded.

eBay fee increases have been steady over the years and aren't likely to reverse. Categories that were profitable at 8% final value fees work differently at 13%. If fees in your categories have increased to a level where your margins don't work, that's a structural problem with selling on eBay in your categories — not an optimization problem you can solve.

Buyer habits are shifting. Younger buyers default to Amazon, TikTok Shop, and social commerce. eBay's core buyer demographic skews older. That's not a crisis — eBay still has over a billion listings and hundreds of millions of buyers — but if your product appeals to an audience that's increasingly shopping elsewhere, diversifying to where those buyers actually are makes sense.

Listing limits and category restrictions can create hard ceilings for sellers who want to scale. If you've hit eBay's selling limits and the platform won't raise them, or if the categories you want to sell in are restricted or prohibited, the only way to grow is to go somewhere else.

Financial Performance Indicators

The numbers that tell you it's time to expand aren't always dramatic. Often it's a slow erosion — margins that were fine two years ago that now require more work for less return. Pay attention to trends, not just current levels.

Declining profit margins are the clearest signal. If you're selling the same volume but keeping less money after fees, shipping, and returns, something structural is changing in your favor. Track net profit per item over time, not just gross revenue.

Revenue can stay flat or even increase while net profit quietly deteriorates.

Revenue plateau despite increasing effort is a meaningful signal. If you've been adding inventory, investing in promoted listings, and optimizing for six months without meaningfully moving sales, you're not doing something wrong — you're hitting a ceiling that additional eBay-specific effort won't raise.

Calculate what you're earning per hour of work. Include everything — sourcing, listing, packing, customer service, returns, accounting. If the number is lower than you'd accept from an employer doing the same work, that's worth knowing. Expanding to more efficient channels or reducing eBay's share of your time may improve the math significantly.

Cash flow problems caused by eBay's payment timing, fund holds, or seasonal fluctuations limit your ability to invest in inventory and growth. If eBay's money management constraints are regularly preventing you from buying good inventory when you find it, other platforms with different payout structures may free up working capital you don't currently have.

When promoted listings are the only thing sustaining visibility and their cost is consuming a meaningful share of your margin, you're effectively paying eBay for access to your own customers. That's a legitimate business model, but it needs to be in your margin calculations — and if it makes the numbers not work, that's information.

Ask what you're giving up by staying exclusively on eBay. The opportunity cost of not listing on Amazon, Etsy, or your own website isn't zero — it's whatever sales you would have made there. That number is unknowable in advance but estimable based on comparable sellers' results on other platforms.

> ▲ **Caution:** Don't expand to new platforms when your eBay business is struggling. Fix operational problems before adding complexity through multi-platform management.

Competitive Landscape Analysis

eBay's competitive landscape has changed structurally in ways that disadvantage smaller sellers. Large operations get volume discounts, better search placement, and access to promotional tools that smaller sellers can't afford. That gap has been widening, not narrowing. Knowing it exists helps you decide where to allocate effort rather than fighting structural disadvantages that optimization alone can't overcome.

Well-funded professional operations entering your categories can undercut prices during market-building phases at a loss, then raise prices once smaller competitors exit. If you're competing against this pattern, winning on price is not a long-term strategy. Competing on knowledge, selection, service, or niche is.

Policy changes consistently favor the infrastructure that large operations can afford. When eBay adds compliance requirements, reporting obligations, or performance standards, small sellers feel the overhead proportionally more than large ones. The burden of staying compliant as policies become more complex is real and growing.

Brand manufacturers selling directly on eBay cut out resellers in categories where they establish a presence. If a brand you've been reselling successfully launches their own eBay store, your listing is now competing directly against the manufacturer who has lower costs, official branding, and manufacturer warranty claims you can't match.

Category consolidation — where one or two dominant sellers control most of the visible inventory in a category — makes profitable entry harder every year. Once consolidation happens, the entrenched sellers have feedback history, sales velocity metrics, and promotional budgets that create a compounding advantage. Finding categories before they consolidate, or niches within consolidated categories, is the opportunity.

Operational Capacity and Resource Assessment

Before you expand, be honest about what you can actually handle. Multi-platform selling isn't inherently harder than single-platform selling, but it is more complex. The answer to "can I do this" isn't optimism — it's an accurate count of the hours you have available, the capital you can allocate, and how much your eBay operations will suffer if some of your attention goes elsewhere.

Time is the real constraint for most sellers. Adding a platform doesn't eliminate the work on the platform you already have — it adds to it. During the learning curve on a new platform, eBay often suffers. Plan for that. Either reduce your eBay inventory load temporarily, get help, or expand during a naturally slower period rather than during your busiest season.

Capital requirements vary significantly by platform. Amazon FBA requires sending inventory to their warehouses, which means buying before you sell. Etsy requires smaller upfront investment. Your own website requires the most capital and the most patience. Match your expansion choice to what your finances can actually support without creating cash flow problems.

Every platform has a learning curve — different listing requirements, different SEO logic, different customer expectations, different policies. Build in time to learn each one properly before expecting it to produce meaningful revenue. Sellers who launch on three platforms simultaneously and do all three poorly would have been better served doing one at a time well.

Your current eBay tools may not extend cleanly to other platforms. Inventory management software, listing tools, and analytics platforms vary in their multi-channel capabilities. Before committing to a new platform, verify that your existing technology either supports it or that you have a plan for managing the gap.

> ■ **Danger Zone:** Never abandon eBay completely before establishing profitable operations on alternative platforms. Maintain your existing revenue while building new channels.

Platform-Specific Expansion Opportunities

The right expansion platform depends entirely on what you sell and who you're selling it to. There's no universally correct answer. The platforms covered in Chapter 26 each have their own character, buyer base, and category strengths — the question is which one overlaps most with your existing inventory and customer profile.

Amazon is the highest-traffic option and the most demanding operationally. The Prime customer base expects speed and reliability that requires either FBA or a very disciplined self-fulfillment operation. The competition is intense and fees are substantial — but for sellers in the right categories, the volume is genuinely transformative.

Social commerce — Facebook Marketplace, Instagram Shopping, TikTok Shop — works for sellers who can create engaging visual content or who have products that benefit from discovery rather than search. These platforms reward sellers who invest in the platform's community format. If you're not willing to engage with that, the traffic won't come.

Niche platforms — Reverb for musical instruments, COMC for sports cards, Chairish for vintage furniture — often have lower traffic than general platforms but buyers who are specifically looking for what you have. Specialization on a niche platform can outperform a broader presence on eBay for the right product categories.

Your own website offers maximum margin and maximum control — and the highest barrier and longest timeline. Building traffic to a direct-to-consumer site from scratch takes years of SEO work, content creation, and customer relationship building. It's worth pursuing as a long-term goal, but don't expect it to replace marketplace income quickly.

Timing and Transition Strategy

Start with one platform, not three. The instinct when recognizing platform dependency risk is to fix it immediately by expanding everywhere at once. That approach usually produces mediocre results on multiple platforms simultaneously rather than a genuinely profitable operation on a single additional channel. Master one before starting the next.

Use eBay's slow seasons to experiment. January through March is typically lower volume for many categories — time you can spend learning a new platform, testing listings, and building initial feedback history without sacrificing peak-season eBay revenue. Mistakes during an experiment phase are cheaper than mistakes during the holidays.

Have financial reserves before you expand. New platforms don't produce revenue immediately. There's a period, weeks to months, where you're investing time and potentially capital without seeing meaningful returns. Expanding from a position of financial stress produces desperate decision-making. Expand from a position of stability and patience.

Track performance on each platform separately. Combined metrics hide what's working and what isn't. A new platform that looks unprofitable in aggregate might be profitable on specific product categories and losing money on others. You can't optimize what you can't see clearly.

Define in advance what success on the new platform looks like and when you'll decide it's not working. "Give it another month" indefinitely is how sellers spend a year on a platform that's not right for their inventory. Set a specific metric threshold — a

certain number of completed sales, a target monthly profit —
and a timeline. Evaluate honestly when you reach it.

Long-term Business Vision and Goals

Expansion decisions are easier when you've already thought
about where you want the business to go. A seller who wants to
build toward a sale needs a different expansion strategy than
one who wants to reduce working hours. A seller focused on
maximum current income expands differently than one focused
on building something that runs without them. Know which of
these you are before you start expanding — different goals
suggest different moves.

Maximum independence from platforms points toward direct-
to-consumer. Your own website, your own customer list, your
own brand. It's the hardest path and the longest timeline, but
it's also the only path that doesn't end with your business
depending on some platform's policy decisions.

Maximum growth points toward Amazon for most product
categories. The traffic is bigger. The customer base is bigger.
The operational demands are bigger. If growth is the goal and
your margins can support the fees, Amazon is the most direct
path to meaningfully larger revenue numbers.

Lifestyle considerations are legitimate strategic factors. A
platform that requires daily shipping and 24-hour response
times is incompatible with extended travel. A platform that
generates irregular income is incompatible with predictable
monthly expenses. Match platform characteristics to how you
actually want to live, not just how much money you want to
make.

The sellers who expand successfully are the ones who do it from
a position of strength — stable eBay operations, financial
reserves, a clear understanding of what they're expanding into
and why. The ones who struggle expand reactively, from

frustration or fear, without the operational foundation that makes new channels work. eBay built your skills. Use those skills to build something that doesn't depend entirely on eBay continuing to be what it is today.

Chapter 28: Long-term Business Strategy

When I first opened my eBay store, I spent hours agonizing over design templates, color schemes, and custom categories. eBay offers dozens of customization options that promise to make your store stand out from competitors and create a professional brand presence.

After several days of tweaking layouts and writing custom descriptions, I realized I was wasting time on activities that generated zero revenue. My customers cared about product photos, accurate descriptions, and fair prices. They didn't care whether my store header matched my brand colors or whether I'd created clever category names.

I abandoned all customization efforts and focused entirely on inventory management and listing optimization. My sales continued growing steadily without any store beautification. The lesson became clear: functionality trumps aesthetics in e-commerce, and time spent on cosmetic improvements could be better invested in sourcing products and improving listings.

This experience taught me to evaluate every business activity based on its direct impact on sales rather than how professional or impressive it might appear to other sellers who probably aren't buying my products anyway.

Long-term strategy for an eBay business sounds like the kind of thing you worry about after you're already making real money. Most sellers never get there — not because the business failed, but because they stayed focused on next month's inventory and never lifted their head to think about what they were actually building. Five years go by doing exactly what they did on day one, just more tired.

The difference between eBay sellers who build something durable and those who just stay busy comes down to one thing: knowing what you're building toward. eBay is a good platform to build from. It's a poor platform to build entirely around. The sellers who figure that out, and act on it, end up with options. The ones who don't end up with a job they can't leave.

Defining Your Business Vision and Mission

Before you can build a long-term strategy, you need to be honest with yourself about what you actually want from this. That sounds obvious, but most sellers never do it. They get caught in the daily grind of listing and shipping and never stop to decide where they're trying to go. Years pass and the business is exactly what it was on day one, just more demanding.

The questions worth asking are simple but uncomfortable. Do you want this to replace your job, or supplement it? Are you building something you could sell someday, or just generating income? What does your life look like when this is going well — and are you actually building toward that, or just reacting to whatever eBay throws at you this week?

Your answers shape everything downstream. A seller who wants to generate $2,000 a month in supplemental income needs a completely different strategy than one who wants to build a business they can hand off or sell. Neither is wrong. But running the wrong strategy for your actual goal is a reliable way to end up frustrated and burned out.

Be realistic about your time and tolerance for stress. eBay can be run as a low-key side business or a demanding full-time operation, but it can't be both at once. Sellers who try to scale aggressively while treating it as a hobby usually end up with the worst of both worlds — too much work to be casual, not enough system to actually scale.

Think about your time horizon too. Building inventory, reputation, and systems takes years. If you need this to work in three months, that pressure will push you toward shortcuts that damage the foundation you're trying to build. Patience isn't a personality trait — it's a strategic requirement.

★ **Pro Tip:** Write a one-page business vision statement that describes where you want your business to be in five years. Use this document to guide major strategic decisions and evaluate new opportunities.

And if you ever want to sell the business or pass it on, that requires building it differently from the start. A business that only runs because you personally know where everything is and how everything works isn't really a business — it's a job you've created for yourself. Real business assets are systems, customer relationships, and brand recognition that function without you standing in the middle of everything.

How you want buyers to see you matters more than most sellers realize. Are you the specialist who knows everything about vintage cameras, or just another person selling whatever they find? Specialists command better prices, earn repeat customers, and build reputations that survive algorithm changes. Generalists compete on price and lose to people with deeper pockets.

Market Evolution and Future Trends

The honest version of eBay's future is this: it will keep getting harder for small sellers. That's not pessimism — it's what happens when any marketplace matures. The casual sellers who made money effortlessly in the early days have mostly left. The ones who stayed either got professional or got squeezed out.

Buyers keep getting more demanding and less forgiving. Amazon trained them to expect miracles, and they bring those expectations to every platform they use. Free shipping, fast delivery, and hassle-free returns aren't perks anymore — they're the floor. Sellers who can't meet that floor don't get second chances.

Technology keeps changing faster than most sellers can adapt. AI-assisted listing tools, automated repricing, and inventory software that syncs across a dozen platforms — these were novelties five years ago and table stakes today. The sellers who treat technology as optional are already falling behind.

Government oversight of online selling keeps expanding. Sales tax used to be something you could mostly ignore. Now eBay collects it automatically in most states, but income reporting requirements and business licensing obligations have gotten more complex, not less. That trend isn't reversing.

And the overseas competition problem isn't going away. Manufacturers who used to sell wholesale to US distributors now sell directly to US consumers, cutting out everyone in the middle. If you're competing on price alone against someone selling the same product from a factory in Shenzhen, you'll lose. The sellers who survive this are the ones who compete on things factories can't easily replicate: expertise, curation, customer relationships, and trust.

Building Sustainable Competitive Advantages

The most durable competitive advantage on eBay isn't price — it's knowledge. Sellers who genuinely know their category buy better, price better, describe better, and answer questions better than generalists who are just trying to move product. That expertise compounds over time. A buyer who trusts you comes back. A buyer who got the best price from whoever had the lowest listing doesn't.

Good supplier relationships give you access to inventory that competitors can't get easily. That might mean an estate sale contact who calls you first, a wholesaler who offers terms once you've proven reliable, or a liquidator who gives regulars first pick. These relationships don't appear overnight — they're built through showing up consistently and being easy to deal with.

Repeat customers are undervalued by most eBay sellers because the platform doesn't make them easy to see. But a buyer who's purchased from you three times is worth more than five new buyers. They already trust you. They skip the competition check. They leave good feedback without being prompted. Build systems that keep track of good customers and give them reasons to come back.

Operational speed matters more than most sellers think. The seller who can list an item in ten minutes, ship same-day, and respond to messages within the hour has a genuine advantage over the seller doing each of those things twice as slowly. Efficiency isn't glamorous, but over time it means more listings, better metrics, and more margin on every sale.

If buyers recognize your store name and associate it with fair deals and honest descriptions, you've built something that algorithms can't easily take away. That kind of recognition takes years, but it's one of the few advantages on eBay that doesn't evaporate the next time the platform changes its fee structure or search ranking criteria.

Financial Planning and Wealth Building

Most eBay sellers reinvest everything back into inventory and never build any financial cushion outside the business. That works until it doesn't — until a suspension, a slow season, or a supplier problem cuts revenue for two months and there's nothing to fall back on. Treat the business like a business: pay yourself, set aside taxes, and keep reserves that aren't tied up in inventory you can't liquidate quickly.

The best thing you can build beyond inventory is a business that has value independent of you showing up every day. Customer lists, a recognized store name, established supplier relationships, documented processes — these are assets. They make the business something you could sell or step back from. Without them, you just have a job that happens to be self-employed.

Don't put everything in eBay. The platform can change its fee structure, suspend your account, or shift algorithms in ways that cut your revenue overnight with no warning and no appeal that actually works. Sellers who built their entire financial lives around a single platform have learned this the hard way. Diversify your income, diversify your investments, and don't let any single company control your financial future.

Get a good accountant who understands e-commerce. The tax situation for online sellers is genuinely complex — self-employment tax, quarterly estimated payments, home office deductions, inventory cost basis — and the mistakes people make trying to handle it themselves are expensive. The cost of professional tax help is a rounding error compared to what you can lose by getting it wrong.

▲ **Caution:** Don't sacrifice long-term financial security for short-term business growth. Maintain personal financial reserves and diversified investments that protect against business failure.

Succession Planning and Exit Strategies

Most eBay sellers never think about exit strategy until they're forced to. That's a mistake, because how you build the business now determines what options you have later. A business that only works because you personally know where everything is, how every supplier relationship works, and how to handle every situation that comes up isn't really a transferable asset — it's a job you've created for yourself. The moment you stop showing up, it stops running.

A business you could actually sell has documented processes, established supplier relationships with contacts beyond just you, a customer base with some history, and performance metrics that tell a buyer what they're getting. Building toward that standard doesn't just serve a future sale — it makes the business more resilient right now, because it means the operations don't depend entirely on you being available and functional every day.

If you're considering an eventual sale, start tracking metrics a buyer would care about: monthly profit (not just revenue), account health history, traffic and conversion data, return rates. A two-year record of consistent profitable performance is worth far more than the same business with no documentation. Buyers price risk, and documentation reduces their perception of it.

Gradual transitions work better than abrupt exits. If you want to reduce your involvement over time — whether for health reasons, retirement, or shifting priorities — building systems and training someone to operate them while you're still present and can fix problems is a much smoother transition than walking away from a business that doesn't yet run without you.

> ■ **Danger Zone:** Don't build businesses that depend entirely on your personal involvement without creating systems and documentation that enable eventual transfer or sale.

Risk Management and Contingency Planning

Risk management for an eBay business is mostly about not having single points of failure. Single platform. Single supplier. Single product category. Single revenue source. Any one of these being disrupted ends or severely damages your business. Building redundancy into each of them is the actual work of risk management — not making a checklist of risks, but actively reducing dependence on any single thing that could break.

Platform dependency is the most obvious risk and the most commonly ignored. eBay can change its fee structure, enforce a policy you didn't realize applied to you, suspend your account over an algorithmic false positive, or shift its algorithm in ways that cut your traffic by half. Any of these can happen without warning and without a reliable appeals process. Sellers on multiple platforms survive eBay problems. Sellers on only eBay don't.

Economic downturns hit eBay sellers unevenly depending on what they sell. Collectibles and vintage items often hold up well during recessions because buyers seek value and nostalgia. Luxury items and high-ticket discretionary goods drop sharply. Know which category your inventory falls into and build cash reserves that can carry you through the slow periods rather than forcing you to liquidate at the worst time.

Health disruption is real and underplanned for. What happens to your eBay business if you can't work for two weeks? For a month? For longer? If the answer is "it falls apart," you have work to do. The minimum viable plan is: vacation mode enabled, handling time set conservatively, and at least one person who knows how to process orders and respond to buyers in an emergency. Building toward more — documented processes, a VA who knows your systems — gives you more options when you need them.

Innovation and Continuous Improvement

The businesses that keep working over time aren't the ones that found the right formula and executed it perfectly forever. They're the ones that kept paying attention and kept adjusting. New product categories when old ones saturated. New tools when better ones emerged. New platforms when eBay changed in ways that made it less attractive for their specific business. The capacity to adapt isn't a personality trait — it's a habit built by making a practice of noticing what's changing before it becomes a crisis.

Ongoing education doesn't require courses or conferences. Reading eBay seller forums, watching what category leaders are doing, paying attention to how buyer behavior in your categories shifts over time — these low-cost habits produce better market intelligence than most formal training. The sellers who get blindsided by changes are usually the ones who stopped paying attention when things were going well.

Measuring Success and Adjusting Strategy

The metrics that tell you whether your strategy is working are simpler than most strategy guides suggest. Are you making more money this year than last year on comparable effort? Is your account healthy? Do you have inventory you're confident in? Are you building toward something, or just maintaining? These questions don't require a KPI dashboard — they require honesty about what you see when you look at the business clearly.

Review what's actually working once a quarter. Not what should be working theoretically — what produced results. Categories that generated good margins. Sourcing approaches that found good inventory. Customer types that turned into repeat buyers. Double down on what works. Cut or deprioritize what doesn't. This is less sophisticated than it sounds, but it's the actual mechanism by which good businesses get better.

Most sellers who build something durable on eBay don't do it by chasing every new opportunity or reacting to every platform change. They do it by knowing what they're building toward, making decisions that serve that direction, and adjusting when the market or the platform changes in ways that require it. That's the whole strategy. It sounds simple because it is — but it requires actually deciding what you're building toward, which most sellers never do.

PART VII: Special Circumstances

Chapter 29: eBay Selling with ADHD

My attempt at dropshipping perfectly illustrated how ADHD can turn promising business opportunities into expensive disasters when enthusiasm outpaces systematic planning and attention to operational details.

I discovered a supplier offering trendy phone accessories at wholesale prices and became convinced I'd found the perfect passive income opportunity. During a hyperfocus session, I created dozens of listings for products I'd never seen, relying entirely on supplier photos and descriptions.

The problems began immediately. Suppliers changed prices without notice, making my listings unprofitable. Shipping times varied wildly, creating angry customers and negative feedback. Product quality didn't match descriptions, leading to returns and disputes. Worst of all, I lost track of which suppliers provided which products, creating fulfillment chaos.

My ADHD brain excelled at spotting the initial opportunity and creating listings quickly, but struggled with the detailed follow-through that dropshipping requires. Inventory tracking, supplier communication, and customer service became overwhelming when problems multiplied faster than I could solve them.

The experience taught me that ADHD entrepreneurs need business models that work with their natural patterns rather than demanding sustained attention to operational details that ADHD brains find tedious and error-prone.

ADHD brains and eBay selling create a relationship more complex than quantum physics and twice as unpredictable. The same neurological wiring that makes traditional employment feel like psychological torture can transform eBay into either the perfect entrepreneurial playground or a spectacular disaster that leaves you surrounded by unsold inventory and half-finished projects.

Knowing how ADHD affects your eBay operations helps you use the unique advantages while developing systems that compensate for the organizational challenges that can derail even the most enthusiastic selling efforts.

ADHD Advantages in eBay Selling

Let's start with what actually works in your favor, because there's real upside here that gets undersold in conversations about ADHD and business.

Hyperfocus is real and it's powerful. When you find a category that captures your interest, you can learn it at a depth and speed that methodical sellers can't match. You'll read every forum post, watch every video, handle every related item at every estate sale. That kind of deep fast learning creates genuine expertise. The trick is directing it toward categories that actually have market demand rather than just ones that interest you personally.

Pattern recognition is another genuine advantage. ADHD minds tend to notice connections that linear thinkers miss — the vintage item that's selling well in one category that would also appeal to buyers in a completely different one, or a price discrepancy between what an item sells for locally versus what it sells for nationally. These intuitive leaps are real business intelligence.

Creative problem-solving shows up in how you photograph awkward items, how you write listings for things that are hard to describe, how you handle the customer service situation that doesn't fit any script. Conventional thinking produces conventional listings. The seller who writes something genuinely interesting or finds an angle no one else thought of tends to stand out.

> ★ **Pro Tip:** Keep a "wins journal" to document your successes and what conditions created them. ADHD brains tend to forget positive patterns while fixating on problems.

Risk tolerance is real too. Starting a business with uncertain income and no guarantee of success requires a comfort with uncertainty that a lot of people genuinely don't have. Many ADHD people find that uncertainty energizing rather than paralyzing — which is actually pretty useful for entrepreneurship.

eBay changes constantly — policies, algorithms, fees, market trends. The sellers who get frustrated by constant change tend to be the ones who prefer stability. If you adapt easily and even enjoy pivoting to new approaches, eBay's instability is less of a burden than it is for your competition.

Interest-driven work produces the best results. When you're genuinely fascinated by what you're selling, it shows in the listings, in the sourcing, in how you talk to buyers. Find categories that genuinely hold your attention — and not just during the initial excitement phase. Categories that keep your interest through the grind are the ones you'll actually build expertise in.

Common ADHD Challenges in eBay Operations

The challenges are just as real as the advantages. Being honest about them — and building systems that account for them — is what separates the ADHD sellers who succeed long-term from the ones who have brilliant starts that fall apart six months in.

Executive function is where eBay gets hard. Listing an exciting new find is easy; systematically processing a pile of thirty medium-interesting items is not. Following through on the routine tasks — responding to messages on a slow Tuesday, updating inventory counts, double-checking a tracking number — is where the ADHD brain tends to slip. These are also exactly the things eBay's algorithm measures.

Time blindness creates real account problems. Missing a shipping deadline because the afternoon disappeared, a genuinely common ADHD experience, counts as a late shipment defect. Delayed customer responses affect your response time metrics. These aren't just inconveniences; they're metric damage that accumulates and eventually triggers eBay enforcement.

Detail errors in listings create return-level problems. The wrong measurements, a missed defect that wasn't photographed, a condition description that doesn't quite match the item — these generate "not as described" returns and defects on your account. A checklist for every listing sounds tedious but it catches the errors that cost money.

Procrastination on boring tasks builds up into crises. The items that need photographing but sit in a corner. The returns that need processing but wait another day. Each one is small but the accumulation creates business problems that are much harder to solve than if they'd been handled when they were fresh.

Difficult buyers hit harder when emotional regulation is already challenged. A frustrating message during a bad focus day can turn into a reactive response that makes the situation worse. Having templates and a rule about not responding to difficult messages until you've had time to calm down is practical self-protection, not just advice.

Overwhelm is the hidden business killer. A busy week with multiple problems happening simultaneously can produce paralysis — nothing gets done because everything feels urgent and impossible to prioritize. Building systems that reduce the number of decisions required during a crisis helps maintain function when the load gets heavy.

Building ADHD-Friendly Business Systems

The goal isn't to function like a neurotypical seller. It's to build systems that get the business results you need while working with how your brain actually operates. Some neurotypical approaches work fine for ADHD sellers. Others are guaranteed failures. Trial and error matters here — what works for someone else may not work for you, and what doesn't work for most sellers might work perfectly for you.

Batch similar tasks into focused work sessions. Photos one afternoon. Listing the next morning. Packing and shipping as a dedicated block. Switching between different types of work is cognitively expensive for ADHD brains — batching reduces that switching cost and makes it easier to get into a productive flow state.

Visual organization beats text-based organization for a lot of ADHD brains. Color-coded bins, items physically sorted by category on a shelf, a whiteboard with the day's tasks written large — these work better than elaborate spreadsheets and app-based systems that require you to remember to check them. Build your workspace to tell you what needs doing, rather than relying on memory to recall it.

Automate the tedious. Automated shipping notifications, templated customer messages, inventory tracking software — anything that runs without requiring your attention is a gift. The fewer routine decisions you have to consciously make, the more mental bandwidth remains for the parts of the business that actually need your judgment.

> ▲ **Caution:** Don't try to force yourself into neurotypical business systems. Build approaches that work with your ADHD brain instead of fighting against it.

External accountability helps. A shipping deadline that exists only in your own mind is easier to miss than one that someone else knows about. An accountability partner, a mastermind group, even just publicly committing to a daily shipment schedule — external pressure gives the ADHD brain a reason to follow through that internal motivation alone sometimes doesn't.

Know your peak hours and protect them for the work that matters most. If your best focus window is 10am to 1pm, that's when you do listings and customer service. Sourcing, packing, and errands can happen during lower-energy windows. Treating all hours as equivalent is a lie the calendar tells — ADHD brains especially need to be honest about when they actually function at different levels.

Build in rewards. ADHD brains are reward-seeking in a way that's more pronounced than average. A small tangible reward after completing a boring batch of tasks — finishing a show, a good snack, a break to look at something interesting — provides the dopamine hit that makes the next task easier to start. This isn't childish; it's working with your neurochemistry.

Inventory Management Strategies for ADHD

Inventory is where ADHD can quietly become expensive. Over-buying during an exciting sourcing trip, then finding stacks of items you can't remember acquiring and haven't listed — this pattern costs money and creates a psychological burden that makes it harder to work in your own space. Keep it manageable.

Simple physical organization beats complex systems. Everything in a dedicated location. Items labeled or bagged when you acquire them. The cost basis written on a piece of masking tape on the item right when you buy it, not reconstructed later from memory. Rely on physical cues in your environment rather than mental notes that evaporate.

Set a buying limit before you go sourcing. Not a vague intention to be reasonable — a specific dollar amount or item count. ADHD hyperfocus at an estate sale can produce a car full of items that seemed individually justified but collectively represent two months of listing backlog. The limit you set before you go is more reliable than the judgment you exercise in the moment.

Capture information immediately. The item you bought, what you paid, where you got it, any condition notes — do this at the point of purchase or immediately after. ADHD working memory is genuinely unreliable for these details over time. Photo the receipt or write it on the item bag in the parking lot. Don't trust the information to still be accessible later.

Schedule inventory reviews as recurring calendar appointments, not open-ended tasks you get to when you remember. Monthly is a reasonable minimum. Pull everything out, confirm you know what you have, and set a listing deadline for anything that's been sitting for more than 60 days. Items that sit too long stop feeling possible to list, which compounds the backlog problem.

Keep sourcing volume aligned with your realistic listing capacity, not your optimistic listing capacity. If you can list twenty items a week sustainably, buy twenty items worth of inventory per sourcing trip — not forty because they were all good finds. The unlisted backlog is money that isn't working.

Customer Service Adaptations

Customer service is the area where ADHD patterns create the most visible account damage. Delayed responses, reactive messages sent in frustration, and inconsistent communication all show up in your metrics. The adaptations here are structural — remove the decision points that ADHD handles poorly rather than trying to willpower through them.

Templates for common messages are mandatory, not optional. Shipping confirmation, response to "where's my item," return acknowledgment, positive feedback request — write these once, make them good, and use them consistently. Having to craft a professional message from scratch when you're frustrated or distracted is a recipe for responses you'll regret.

Set specific message-checking times rather than monitoring constantly. Two or three defined windows per day — morning, midday, evening — are better than checking every twenty minutes between tasks. Constant availability fragments focus. Defined response windows preserve it, and as long as you respond within 24 hours you're meeting eBay's standard.

Have a rule about difficult messages: don't respond until you've cooled down. Even fifteen minutes between reading a frustrating message and replying to it makes a significant difference in the quality of the response. ADHD emotional reactivity is real and it's faster than the part of your brain that knows what a good customer service response looks like.

Write out a decision tree for returns and complaints. When a buyer says X, the response is Y. When they say Z, the response is W. Having this written down means that when you're overwhelmed and can't think clearly, you follow the flowchart rather than improvising. Pre-made decisions are more reliable than real-time judgment under stress.

Know your own limits and plan around them. If you have predictable low-functioning periods — afternoons, certain days, high-stress weeks — either reduce eBay volume during those periods or have a backup arrangement. A trusted person who can handle time-sensitive responses for a day when you genuinely can't is worth identifying before you need them.

Don't over-promise during hyperfocus peaks. Same-day shipping, unusually fast responses, special accommodations offered in enthusiasm — these become obligations that future-you has to fulfill when the energy isn't there. Set your handling time at a level your worst days can meet, not your best days.

Time Management and Scheduling

ADHD time management is less about following a system and more about building an environment that compensates for the brain's natural blind spots. Time blindness — the genuine inability to feel time passing or accurately estimate how long things take — isn't a character flaw. It's a neurological feature. External structures substitute for the internal time sense that's unreliable.

Know which hours you actually function at different levels. Most ADHD brains have a clear window of peak executive function — usually a few hours, not all day. High-stakes tasks go in that window. Customer service responses, listing quality checks, anything requiring attention to detail. Low-stakes tasks — packing, organizing, watching pricing data — go elsewhere.

Time blocks with visible timers work better than schedules for many ADHD brains. Knowing you have 45 minutes to list items — and watching a timer count down — creates urgency that internal scheduling doesn't. The Pomodoro technique (25 minutes on, 5 off) works well for some; others do better with longer blocks. Experiment to find your own rhythm.

Build buffer time into every deadline. If shipping must go out by 5pm, your personal deadline is 3pm. If an order needs to be placed by Tuesday, your internal deadline is Monday. The ADHD brain routinely encounters unexpected distractions, hyperfocus diversions, and time-disappearing episodes. Build for them rather than assuming they won't happen.

> ■ **Danger Zone:** Don't ignore ADHD medication effects on business performance. Stimulant medications can improve focus but may affect risk assessment and emotional regulation.

Routines reduce decision fatigue. A consistent daily sequence for business tasks — same order, same time, same trigger cues — means each task starts automatically rather than requiring a separate decision to begin. The less deciding required, the more energy available for the tasks themselves. Build variety into the tasks, not into the routine structure.

Scheduled breaks are mandatory, not optional. ADHD brains that skip breaks to "finish up" often hit a wall that costs more time than the break would have. Build them in deliberately. The productivity math on breaks is counterintuitive but real — working 45 minutes and taking 10 off repeatedly produces more than grinding for four hours straight and then being useless.

Prioritize by consequences, not interest. ADHD brains naturally gravitate toward the most interesting task, which is often not the most important one. Shipping deadlines have consequences. Listing optimization is interesting but not urgent. Train yourself to ask "what breaks if I don't do this today?" and start there — every day, before you do what you want to do.

Financial Management Considerations

ADHD financial management problems are usually structural, not moral. Impulsive buying, present-bias spending, optimism about income, underestimating future costs — these are predictable patterns. The solution isn't trying harder not to do them. It's building systems that route around them.

Set buying budgets before sourcing trips and treat them as fixed. Not "I'll aim to spend around this much" but "I have exactly this much in my sourcing account and when it's gone the trip is over." Physical cash or a dedicated debit card with a loaded amount works better than mental limits applied at the point of purchase.

Separate business and personal finances completely — different bank accounts, different cards, different mental categories. The boundary reduces the chance that a bad personal week bleeds into business spending, and makes it much clearer whether the business is actually profitable. Commingled finances make both categories harder to manage.

Automate tax savings. When eBay pays out, a percentage — 25–30% is reasonable for US sellers — should immediately transfer to a separate tax account before it's available to spend. ADHD present-focus will spend money that exists. Removing it from the available balance before the spending decision happens eliminates the problem.

A bookkeeper or accountant is worth the cost. Not just for tax preparation — for monthly oversight that creates the external accountability ADHD financial management needs. Knowing someone is going to review your numbers next month changes how you treat them this month.

Capture tax-relevant information throughout the year. Mileage, receipts, cost basis — document it at the time or it disappears. A simple app for mileage tracking, a folder (physical or digital) for receipts, a spreadsheet row added after every purchase. The annual reconstruction of a year's worth of business activity is a genuinely miserable task that ADHD sellers especially dread. Make it unnecessary.

Keep an emergency fund. ADHD optimism about income consistency is a feature of the condition, not a realistic planning tool. Slow sales months, unexpected returns, equipment failures, eBay holds — these happen. Three months of operating expenses as a reserve means these events are inconveniences rather than crises.

ADHD Creativity and Innovation as Competitive Advantage

The systems and structures discussed throughout this chapter exist to protect the business from ADHD's downsides. This section is about the upsides — the parts that, if you can channel them effectively, create genuine competitive advantages that more methodical sellers can't easily replicate.

The ADHD eye for unusual items is a real sourcing advantage. The ability to notice something that doesn't fit — the piece in the wrong category at a thrift store, the item being sold by someone who doesn't know what it is — produces finds that patient, systematic buyers miss. Use it. It's one of the places where your brain works in your favor without needing a system to compensate.

Creative listing presentations stand out. Most eBay listings are competent and dull. The seller who writes a title that actually communicates something interesting, or a description with a personality, or photographs that tell a story — these listings get clicks. ADHD can make the listing process tedious, but the individual listings themselves can be genuinely better if you allow yourself to bring something creative to them.

Trend spotting is genuine value. The wide-ranging interest patterns that ADHD often produces — knowing a little about a lot of things — means you can spot crossover demand before it's obvious. The item that's appreciated in one community that another community would love too. The category that's emerging before the YouTube resellers discover it and tell everyone.

Deep niche expertise is where ADHD hyperfocus produces its most defensible business value. When you've spent 200 hours reading about a specific category because you genuinely couldn't stop — the identification guides, the collector forums, the auction history — you know things that casual sellers don't. That knowledge shows in your listings, your pricing, and your ability to authenticate and describe items accurately.

ADHD enthusiasm is infectious when directed at things you genuinely care about. Buyers notice when a seller actually loves what they're selling. It shows in the description, in the photos, in the willingness to answer questions in detail. That authentic engagement is something you can't manufacture if it isn't there — and with ADHD, when you find the right category, it's usually very much there.

ADHD and eBay is a combination that can go either direction — brilliant and profitable or chaotic and expensive — depending primarily on whether you understand your own patterns well enough to build systems that protect against the downsides while the advantages do their work. The people who figure this out tend to be unusually good at this business. The people who don't tend to have very exciting first three months followed by a pile of unsold inventory and a suspended account.

eBay selling works unusually well for many people with disabilities — not as a compromise or a lesser option, but because the structural features of the business align naturally with what disability often requires. No fixed hours. No commute. No supervisor deciding whether your accommodation request is reasonable. You control the workspace, the schedule, and the pace.

This chapter covers both the genuine advantages — the ways eBay's model maps well onto disability realities — and the practical challenges that need real solutions, not just encouragement. The goal is a business designed around your actual capacity, not an idealized version of it.

Accessibility Advantages in eBay Operations

The structural features of eBay selling map remarkably well onto what many disabled people need from work. No fixed location, no required hours, no office environment to navigate, no supervisor who makes accommodation decisions. You control the workspace, the schedule, and the physical setup. That's genuinely unusual for income-generating work, and it's worth naming directly.

Medical appointments, treatment schedules, energy fluctuations, symptom flares — none of these require you to call anyone or justify anything. You set your own handling time. You choose your own listing volume. On a good day you do more; on a bad day you do less. The business absorbs that variability in a way that traditional employment mostly can't.

There's no performance review where someone decides whether your pace is acceptable. No HR process when you need a different kind of chair or a different kind of lighting. You optimize your workspace for your actual needs, not for whatever the facility manager permits. That autonomy has concrete value for people whose needs are specific and non-standard.

Physical demands are modifiable. eBay doesn't require standing, commuting, lifting beyond what you choose to source, or maintaining a specific pace. The physical requirements of the business are largely determined by what you sell and how you choose to handle it. Sellers with mobility limitations, chronic pain, or stamina constraints can build operations that work within their actual capacity rather than someone else's assumption of it.

> ★ **Pro Tip:** Document your business expenses for disability-related equipment and modifications. Many assistive technology costs qualify as business deductions when used for eBay operations.

Assistive technology works for eBay. Voice recognition for listing creation, screen readers for managing orders and messages, specialized keyboards or input devices for sellers with limited dexterity, text-to-speech for monitoring feedback — the platform's primarily text-based interface is compatible with a wide range of accessibility tools in ways that many physical jobs aren't.

Selling what genuinely interests you is available to everyone, but it matters especially when your capacity to pivot and hustle is limited by health. Deep expertise in a specific category — built through genuine interest rather than profit calculation — creates listings and customer service that distinguish you from sellers who are just moving product. That expertise is sustainable in a way that grinding through unfamiliar categories isn't.

Common Accessibility Challenges and Solutions

Physical limitations need practical solutions for the operational parts of eBay selling — inventory management, photography, packing, and shipping. Most of these have solutions; the key is designing the workflow around your actual capacity from the start rather than trying to adapt a workflow designed for able-bodied operation.

Storage and workspace setup should be organized for your body, not for conventional efficiency. Adjustable shelving, rolling carts that eliminate carrying, items sorted so the most frequently handled ones are at the most accessible height. These aren't accommodations — they're just good workspace design that happens to matter more when physical capacity is limited.

Photography is one of the most adaptable parts of eBay selling. A tripod eliminates the need to hold a camera steady. Remote shutter triggers mean no bending or stretching to reach the button. A lightbox positioned at the right height means the photography station works rather than the seller working around it. Photo setup is worth investing time in once — it pays back every time you list.

Packaging and shipping modifications help manage weight restrictions and repetitive motion concerns through ergonomic workstations, shipping services that provide pickup, and packaging solutions that reduce physical demands.

Voice recognition software enables listing creation and customer communication when typing becomes difficult due to arthritis, carpal tunnel, or other conditions affecting manual dexterity.

Conditions that affect energy, concentration, or cognitive function benefit from the same organizational approaches: checklists that reduce reliance on memory, automated reminders, simplified workflows that minimize decision points. The goal is reducing the mental load of the operational parts of the business so your cognitive capacity goes toward things that actually require it.

Vision accessibility tools work well with eBay's platform. Screen magnification, high-contrast display settings, and text-to-speech for reading messages and order details are all available. The listing interface can be navigated primarily through keyboard rather than mouse. Visually impaired sellers who want to work through specific accessibility challenges with eBay's platform are often surprised by how much is already supported.

Energy Management Strategies

Fluctuating energy is one of the most common features of chronic illness and disability, and it's the feature that conventional employment handles worst. eBay handles it much better — but only if you design the business for your energy reality rather than for an imagined version of yourself that functions at full capacity every day.

Spoon theory — the framework that treats energy as a finite daily resource that gets spent on every activity — is useful for eBay planning. Which business tasks cost the most energy? Which ones can be done on low-energy days? Which ones require a good day to do well? Understanding your own energy map makes business planning more realistic and prevents the pattern of good days prompting overcommitment that creates bad weeks.

When energy is limited, prioritize by consequence. What breaks if it doesn't get done today? Shipping deadlines and time-sensitive customer messages have real consequences. Optimizing listings and researching new categories can wait. Protecting your account metrics — by ensuring the most critical tasks get done even on difficult days — matters more than squeezing extra productivity out of good days.

Batch similar tasks to minimize cognitive switching cost. Processing all pending messages at once costs less energy than switching between listing, messaging, and packing repeatedly. Batching also means that if you only have one good window of function in a day, you can apply it entirely to the highest-priority task category rather than spreading it thin.

Automate whatever can be automated. Shipping notifications, message templates, repricing tools — anything that runs without requiring your energy is a resource that doesn't deplete. The goal is a business where the minimum viable activity to maintain account health requires as little energy as possible, so that your best days produce improvement and your worst days don't produce damage.

Plan for flares before they happen. What happens to your business if you can't function for a week? Having a plan — trusted person with access to handle time-sensitive tasks, vacation mode turned on in your store, handling time set conservatively enough to absorb gaps — means a health crisis is a setback rather than a business-ending event.

> ▲ **Caution:** Don't overcommit during good days. Sustainable businesses account for disability fluctuations rather than assuming peak performance will continue indefinitely.

Pace yourself on good days. The temptation during high-energy periods is to make up for lost time — listing twice as many items, taking on extra complexity, committing to faster handling times. This pattern produces boom-bust cycles where overexertion on good days creates extended recovery periods that disrupt the consistency eBay requires. Sustainable steady beats sporadic intense.

Financial Benefits and Considerations

The financial picture for disabled sellers on eBay involves some real complexity that deserves honest attention rather than vague optimism. eBay income can supplement disability benefits — but the interaction with SSDI, SSI, and other programs has specific rules, thresholds, and reporting requirements that vary by program. Getting this wrong can jeopardize benefits you depend on.

Social Security has specific work incentives for self-employed disabled individuals, including the Trial Work Period and the Substantial Gainful Activity threshold. These are real programs with real benefits — but navigating them requires accurate information, not general advice. Contact your local Social Security office or a benefits counselor before your eBay income reaches levels that might affect your eligibility.

If your health insurance comes through Medicaid, Medicare, or ACA marketplace plans tied to income, be aware that business income affects premium calculations and eligibility. This isn't a reason not to build the business — it's a reason to plan for the transitions rather than be surprised by them.

Disability-related business expenses are often deductible. Assistive technology used for the business, workspace modifications, accessibility equipment — these reduce your taxable income. Document them carefully and discuss them with a tax professional who understands both self-employment and disability-related deductions.

Emergency funds matter more for disabled sellers than for most. Higher medical costs, potential income gaps during health crises, equipment failures at inconvenient times — these are predictable occurrences that need financial buffers. Build reserves as a deliberate business strategy, not an afterthought.

Technology and Assistive Equipment

The technology toolkit for disabled eBay sellers has expanded significantly. Most barriers that required workarounds a decade ago have direct solutions now. The key is investing in what actually helps your situation rather than accumulating tools you don't use.

Input device alternatives are worth experimenting with if standard keyboard and mouse are difficult. Ergonomic keyboards, trackball mice, one-handed keyboards, voice recognition, eye-tracking input — the right tool for your specific situation is often not the default tool. Most can be tested before committing to a purchase.

Mobile devices have made managing eBay operations from bed, a wheelchair, or anywhere else with connectivity genuinely practical. The eBay seller app handles most critical tasks. If sitting at a desk is difficult or impossible, mobile management is a real option rather than a compromise.

Shipping is one of the most physically demanding parts of eBay selling and one of the most modifiable. USPS, UPS, and FedEx all offer free home or business pickup. Online label printing eliminates trips to the post office entirely. Pre-paid label services, packaging supply delivery, and carrier pickup scheduling are all free or low-cost and eliminate most of the heavy lifting and travel that shipping otherwise requires.

Customer service is entirely text-based on eBay. For sellers with speech difficulties or hearing impairments, the platform's communication model is already perfectly compatible — written messages, no phone calls required. This is one area where eBay's design incidentally works better for many disabled sellers than in-person retail ever could.

> ■ **Danger Zone:** Don't let disability pride prevent you from using helpful accommodations or assistive technology. Business success matters more than proving you can do everything without help.

Building Disability-Friendly Business Systems

Design the business for the body and mind you actually have. This sounds obvious but it's the step most people skip — they build a business that would work fine for a healthy person and then try to adapt it when it doesn't. Starting with your actual constraints produces a more sustainable result than retrofitting accommodations after the fact.

Simplify ruthlessly. Every additional step in a process is a potential point of failure on a bad day. Checklists replace memory. Templates replace real-time writing. Automation replaces manual monitoring. The simpler the operational system, the more reliably it runs when you're not at full capacity.

Have a written emergency plan. Who can handle time-sensitive eBay tasks if you can't? What's the process for putting the store on vacation mode? What auto-messages go out? How do pending orders get handled? Write this down when you're well, because you will need it when you aren't, and the time you're least able to figure it out is also when it will matter most.

Build support before you need it. A family member who knows your systems well enough to help in a crisis. A friend who can drop packages for you. A VA familiar enough with your templates to handle basic customer service. These relationships take time to establish; don't wait until you're hospitalized to start building them.

Keep documentation in accessible formats. Instructions written in plain language, stored somewhere findable, not in your head. If cognitive difficulties affect you on some days, you need your documentation to be usable on those days, not just on your best ones.

Disability Community and Networking

Disability communities often include people who have already figured out versions of the challenges you're facing — accessible workspace setups, benefits navigation, assistive technology that actually works, strategies for managing a business through flares. Connecting with these communities provides practical information that general business advice doesn't address.

Disabled seller communities specifically — on Reddit, Facebook groups, disability-focused business forums — connect people who understand both the eBay side and the disability side. These connections are worth finding because someone who navigated the same intersection of problems you're facing has already learned the hard lessons you haven't encountered yet.

Disability communities are also niche markets. Adaptive equipment, mobility aids, assistive technology, accessible home modifications — if you have direct experience with these products and their quality varies significantly, you may be better positioned than any other seller to evaluate, source, and describe them accurately. That kind of expertise-driven sourcing is exactly what builds a defensible niche.

Legal Protections and Rights

The legal landscape for disabled business owners includes protections and benefits that are worth knowing about, though the specifics require professional guidance to apply correctly to your situation.

The ADA requires businesses and service providers to make reasonable accommodations. This applies to the service providers you use as a business owner — shipping carriers, financial institutions, business service companies. If a standard process creates a genuine access barrier for you, you have the right to request accommodation, and most providers have processes for this.

Tax credits exist for disabled business owners who make accessibility improvements or hire disabled employees. The specifics vary; a tax professional familiar with disability-related deductions and credits is the right resource for identifying what applies to your situation.

Business insurance for disabled sellers should account for health-related business interruption. Standard business interruption insurance covers disasters and events — not personal illness. If your business depends on your personal capacity to operate and that capacity is variable, understanding what your insurance does and doesn't cover is worth doing proactively.

Benefits counselors — available through Social Security and some disability organizations — specialize in helping disabled people navigate the complex interaction between work and benefits. They understand the rules specific to your benefit type and can help you plan income levels and business structure to optimize your situation legally. Use them before making income decisions, not after.

Building Sustainable Success

Sustainability here means building a business that functions across your actual range of capacity — not just the good days. Set goals calibrated to your realistic productive capacity rather than your peak capacity. The business that earns steadily at a sustainable pace creates more actual income than the one that sprints during good periods and collapses during bad ones.

Growth is possible — but grow within your actual capacity, not your aspirational capacity. Bringing in a VA for specific tasks, shifting to lower-maintenance inventory, building systems that reduce daily demands — these create growth that doesn't break when your health fluctuates. Scaling by adding volume without changing systems usually produces more stress rather than more income.

eBay selling offers genuine opportunity for financial independence for disabled people — not as a workaround or a lesser option, but as a business model that happens to align well with what many disabled people actually need from work. The flexibility, the location independence, the technology compatibility, the self-determination — these are structural features that work in your favor when you design the business around your reality. That's not accommodation. That's good business design.

Chapter 31: Using Virtual Assistants and Outsourced Resources

Virtual assistants promise to transform your eBay business from a one-person operation into a scalable enterprise while you focus on high-level strategy and profit optimization. The reality involves managing people you've never met who work in different time zones and may have vastly different ideas about quality standards and business priorities than you do.

Successful outsourcing requires understanding which tasks benefit from delegation versus those that demand your personal attention while developing management systems that make sure remote workers actually improve your business instead of creating expensive new problems.

Identifying Tasks Suitable for Outsourcing

The question isn't "what can a VA do" — the answer is almost anything procedural. The question is "what tasks in my business are taking time away from things only I can do, and can those tasks be documented clearly enough that someone else can do them reliably." If you can't document it, you can't delegate it successfully.

Listing creation works well when you have clear templates, a product information format, and quality standards that are specific enough to evaluate. A VA who can follow a thorough listing template will produce consistent results. A VA who has to guess what you want will produce inconsistent ones. The template quality matters more than the VA quality for this task.

Research tasks — competitor pricing, market data, trend monitoring — are good candidates if you can define exactly what you're looking for and in what format. "Research products to sell" is not delegatable without much more specificity. "Check completed sales on eBay for these 10 items and report average selling price and sell-through rate in this spreadsheet format" is.

Routine customer service works with a VA if your templates cover the common scenarios and your escalation rules are clear. "Where is my order" questions, return acknowledgments, positive feedback requests — these are high-volume, low-judgment tasks that a VA with good English and attention to detail can handle reliably. Complex disputes, unhappy buyers, anything requiring judgment — those stay with you.

Data entry, spreadsheet maintenance, inventory tracking updates — these are the tasks that take your time without requiring your expertise. If it's updating a column in a spreadsheet or recording information from eBay reports into a tracking document, a VA can do it. If it requires you to interpret what you're looking at and make a decision, keep it.

★ **Pro Tip:** Start by outsourcing one specific task and perfect that workflow before adding additional responsibilities. Trying to delegate too much too fast usually creates chaos.

Photo editing — background removal, color correction, sizing to eBay specifications — is genuinely delegatable if you have clear standards and a reliable workflow for getting images to and from the VA. If your photos already require work before they get to editing, that earlier work usually stays with you.

Social media management is delegatable if you're doing it at all and have established brand guidelines. Most small eBay sellers haven't reached the point where social media management is worth outsourcing — it requires more audience and more content than most sellers have. If you're at that point, it follows the same rule: document the standards clearly enough that someone else can meet them.

Finding and Vetting Quality Virtual Assistants

Finding a good VA requires actual screening, not just reviewing profiles and picking someone who sounds promising. Freelance platforms are full of VAs who will tell you whatever gets them hired. Test before committing.

The major freelance platforms — Upwork, Fiverr, OnlineJobs.ph, and others — each attract different pools of candidates with different skill levels and rate expectations. OnlineJobs.ph focuses specifically on Filipino VAs and tends to have lower rates and stronger English than general freelance platforms. Upwork has more built-in accountability tools. Neither is universally better; the right platform depends on what you need.

Give candidates a paid test task before hiring. Tell them to list a specific item using your template, respond to a specific customer inquiry using your guidelines, or research a specific market question and present the findings. What they produce tells you more than their entire work history. The cost of the test task is negligible compared to the cost of hiring the wrong person and discovering the problem after they've had access to your business for a month.

Look at feedback from previous clients, but read it critically. Generic praise tells you little. Specific feedback about the type of work, reliability, and how problems were handled tells you much more. References from clients who worked with the VA on eBay-related tasks specifically are more valuable than generic positive reviews.

During initial conversations, observe response time and communication quality. A VA who takes three days to answer your first message before being hired won't magically become more responsive after. One whose messages require significant translation or interpretation effort will create the same friction throughout the working relationship. Communication quality in the hiring process predicts communication quality on the job.

Start small. Give a new VA one specific, bounded task with a clear output. Evaluate the result. If it's good, add another task. If it's not, you've spent a small amount of money on a test rather than a large amount of money on a problem. The sellers who have bad VA experiences usually hired too fast and gave too much responsibility before establishing trust through demonstrated performance.

Setting Up Effective Management Systems

VA management quality depends almost entirely on how well you document what you want. The VA is not telepathic. They can't replicate your judgment or fill in gaps with their own expertise. Everything they need to do the job correctly has to be written down, specific, and testable. If a procedure isn't documented, it won't be done consistently.

Standard operating procedures for every task you delegate. Each SOP should cover: what the task is, what a good result looks like, what to do when something doesn't fit the template, and who to ask when they're uncertain. Screen record yourself doing the task once and narrate it — this creates a video SOP that's often clearer than written instructions alone.

Training is onboarding, not a one-time event. A VA who works with your business for a month will encounter situations not covered in the initial training. Build a culture of questions rather than guessing — you want them to ask when unsure rather than produce wrong work and say nothing. "If you're not sure, ask before proceeding" should be an explicit instruction, not an assumption.

Regular check-ins — brief daily or every-other-day messages — maintain coordination without becoming micromanagement. What did you complete? What's in progress? What's blocking you? This cadence surfaces problems early when they're small rather than discovering them when they've compounded into bigger issues.

> ▲ **Caution:** Never give VAs access to your eBay account passwords or financial information. Use role-based permissions and separate accounts when possible.

Sample work before it goes live. Don't review the listing after it's published — review it before you approve it. Build a quality check step into the process for any task that has customer-facing output. A listing with an error that went live created a problem you now have to fix; a listing with an error caught during review took thirty seconds to correct.

Track what actually gets done against what was assigned. This doesn't require elaborate software — a simple shared spreadsheet where tasks are listed and checked off as completed creates visibility into patterns. A VA who consistently misses the same type of task or consistently produces lower quality on specific work tells you something that casual observation won't reveal.

Give VAs access to only what they need. Create a separate eBay account with limited seller permissions for VAs who manage listings. Use a separate email address for VA-managed communications. Never share your main account credentials. If a VA's access is compromised or they leave badly, the blast radius should be limited.

Task-Specific Outsourcing Strategies

Different tasks have different delegation risk profiles. The higher the judgment required and the more directly customer-facing the output, the more careful the oversight needs to be.

Listing creation is the most commonly delegated task and works well with strong templates. The VA fills in information using your format; you review before publishing. The time savings are real. The risk is listings that don't match your quality standards, which is a quality control problem, not a delegation problem. Review the first twenty listings from any new VA before establishing a lighter-touch review process.

Research tasks work when the criteria are specific and the output format is defined. A VA who reports "these 10 items have sold for an average of X over the past 90 days with Y% sell-through" has produced useful information. A VA who reports "lots of things are selling" has produced nothing useful. The quality of your specification determines the quality of the research output.

Customer service delegation requires the most careful oversight because poor responses can damage buyer relationships, generate bad feedback, and create eBay policy violations under your account. Templates and clear escalation rules are non-negotiable. Any message that doesn't fit the template goes to you before the VA sends it.

Inventory management support — updating tracking spreadsheets, recording cost basis, maintaining inventory counts — is low-judgment and highly delegatable. The key is that your VA records information; you make decisions about what to do with that information. Never delegate purchasing, pricing, or strategic inventory decisions to a VA.

Administrative tasks — calendar management, file organization, basic email filtering — are good candidates for delegation if they're genuinely consuming your time. Many small eBay sellers overestimate how much time these tasks actually take versus how much time the management overhead of a VA adds. Do the actual math before outsourcing administrative work.

Communication and Cultural Considerations

Most eBay sellers who use VAs work with international contractors, most commonly from the Philippines, India, or other countries with English-proficient workforces and competitive rates. The cultural and communication dynamics of these relationships are different from domestic employees, and getting them wrong is one of the most common reasons VA relationships fail.

Written instructions are more reliable than verbal or video instructions alone because they're referenceable. Even excellent English speakers miss things in long verbal explanations that they would catch in written form. And written instructions with screenshots or examples are more reliable still. Invest time in creating good written documentation; it reduces miscommunication and training time for every future VA.

Time zone differences require planning. A VA in the Philippines working your evening is working their morning. Feedback that arrives at 10pm your time gets a response at their 9am. Turnaround on corrections or questions typically takes a full day-cycle rather than an hour. Build this into your workflows rather than expecting real-time collaboration that the time difference makes structurally impossible.

■ **Danger Zone:** Don't assume VAs understand American business culture or eBay policies. Provide explicit training about expectations, ethics, and platform requirements.

Some cultures have stronger norms around deference to authority that mean a VA may not volunteer that something isn't working or that they don't understand an instruction. Create explicit permission to raise concerns and ask questions: "If something doesn't make sense or you run into a situation not covered by the instructions, please message me before proceeding." This needs to be stated, not assumed.

Know your VA's holidays. Philippines, India, and other countries have different national holidays than the US — some of which may not be on your radar. A week when eBay sales are picking up during a US holiday period may coincide with your VA's own holidays. Communicate about upcoming absences in advance rather than discovering the coverage gap when it happens.

Treat VAs professionally and fairly. Pay rates that reflect the work quality you expect. Provide feedback that's specific and constructive. Acknowledge good work. The VAs who get the best performance from their contractors are usually the ones who treat the relationship like a professional partnership — because that's what it is.

Cost-Benefit Analysis and Budgeting

The most common mistake with VA hiring is underestimating the total cost. The VA's hourly rate is only part of it. Add your time creating documentation, onboarding, reviewing work, managing the relationship, and correcting mistakes. A VA who costs $8/hour but requires two hours of management per day to produce results you could have done yourself in three hours saved you nothing.

The math only works if the VA frees up your time for higher-value work. If you're delegating listing creation so you can do more sourcing — and more sourcing generates more profit than the VA costs — the economics work. If you're delegating listing creation and then spending the freed time watching Netflix, you've added overhead without adding value. The VA's value is what you do with the time you recover.

Quality impact is a real cost. A VA who produces below-standard listings, customer service messages that damage buyer relationships, or research that leads to bad purchasing decisions costs more than what you pay them. Measure quality outcomes, not just task completion.

Scale VA usage as business grows. The break-even point on VA investment moves as volume increases. At 50 listings a month, VA-assisted listing creation may not be worth it. At 500 a month, it almost certainly is. Revisit the calculation periodically rather than assuming whatever you decided last year is still right.

Risk budget for mistakes. VAs make errors — listing errors that create returns, customer service responses that generate complaints, research that leads you to bad inventory. Budget for some error rate and build review systems to minimize it. The question isn't whether errors will happen; it's whether your oversight is good enough that errors get caught before they cost real money.

Managing Multiple Virtual Assistants

Multiple VAs are appropriate when you have multiple distinct workflows that each benefit from dedicated focus, not when you want to duplicate the same work across multiple people. One VA who does listings well, another who handles customer service, another who manages research — this is specialization that makes sense. Three VAs all doing similar listing work creates coordination overhead without proportional benefit.

Clear role boundaries are essential. Each VA needs to know exactly what's their responsibility and what isn't. Overlap creates "I thought they were handling that" gaps. Define roles with enough specificity that there's no ambiguity about who owns which task and who the escalation point is for edge cases.

A shared project management tool — Asana, Trello, Notion, a simple shared spreadsheet — tracks task assignments and status across the team. This is less about surveillance and more about preventing things from falling through the cracks when you have multiple people all moving simultaneously on different parts of the business.

Legal and Security Considerations

VA relationships create real legal and security obligations that many sellers skip until they've had a bad experience. Address them before you start, not after something goes wrong.

Use a written contractor agreement. It doesn't need to be elaborate, but it should cover: work scope, payment terms, confidentiality requirements, who owns work product created by the VA, and termination terms. A simple agreement that both parties sign protects you if the relationship ends badly and establishes clear expectations from the start.

Your VA has access to some of your business data — listing information, customer interactions, perhaps pricing data. Keep that access limited to what they actually need and use separate credentials wherever possible. If a VA is removed from your team, change the passwords for any systems they had access to. This is basic operational hygiene, not suspicion.

Work product created by a contractor belongs to the employer unless specified otherwise — but this should be explicit in your agreement, not assumed. Templates, listing copy, and research documents your VA creates should clearly belong to your business. This matters if you ever bring a similar business task in-house or if a VA attempts to reuse your proprietary content elsewhere.

US sellers paying international contractors don't typically withhold taxes, but they may have 1099 filing obligations for domestic contractors above certain payment thresholds. International payments have different rules. Ask your accountant about contractor payment reporting before you make significant payments rather than sorting it out during tax season.

Everything your VA does on your eBay account is your responsibility. eBay doesn't recognize that a VA created a problematic listing or sent a policy-violating message on your behalf. Train your VA on eBay's relevant policies explicitly; don't assume they know them. Verify their work before it goes live.

VA outsourcing can genuinely scale an eBay business in ways that aren't possible with one person doing everything. The sellers who get this right are usually the ones who put in the documentation and management work upfront — the SOPs, the quality checks, the clear communication. The ones who get it wrong usually tried to skip that work and discovered that undocumented delegation produces undocumented results.

Conclusion

eBay in 2025 is not the platform most of us fell in love with. The auction site that felt like a community — where you could list something on a whim and find someone who genuinely wanted it, where the feedback system made strangers trustworthy, where the whole thing had a kind of scrappy magic to it — that place is mostly gone. What replaced it is a corporate marketplace that prioritizes its own metrics and treats sellers as one of several revenue streams to be optimized.

It's worth naming that loss honestly, because it changes what success means. Building a profitable eBay business in 2025 requires treating it as a professional operation — understanding the algorithm, managing your metrics, protecting your account, watching your margins, adapting to policy changes that don't always make sense. It requires the kind of attention and systems that casual selling never did.

But the opportunity is still there. The platform still has hundreds of millions of buyers. The search traffic is still organic — you don't have to build an audience. The infrastructure for connecting a seller with a specific item to a buyer who wants exactly that item still works, and it still works better than most alternatives for the kinds of things that have always sold well on eBay: used goods, vintage items, specialized equipment, collectibles, things you can source locally and ship nationally.

The specific advice in this book will drift as eBay continues changing its policies and algorithms. That drift is inevitable — it's been happening since 1995. What doesn't change is the underlying logic: understand your costs, describe things accurately, ship fast, treat buyers well, protect your account health, and don't depend on any single platform for your entire livelihood. Those principles outlast any particular set of eBay rules.

I've been selling on eBay since 2003. I've watched it go through more transformations than most sellers bother counting. Some of those changes hurt. Some of the things that made the early platform special are genuinely gone, and I miss them. But I've also had thousands of transactions with buyers I'd never have reached any other way — people who wanted exactly what I had, who were grateful for honest descriptions and careful packing, who left feedback that felt like a real acknowledgment rather than a metric. Those moments still happen. They just require more work to find.

What this book tried to give you is an honest picture of what that work actually involves — not a motivational promise that eBay is easy, and not a cynical argument that it's hopeless. The truth is somewhere in the middle, and it's different for every seller depending on what they're selling, how much time they have, and what kind of business they're trying to build.

Go build something. The platform is complicated, the margins are tighter than they used to be, and some days eBay will make you want to list your inventory somewhere else entirely. But somewhere out there, there's a buyer who wants exactly what's sitting in your garage. That's still worth something.

About the Author

Richard has been selling on eBay since 2003, when the platform still resembled a digital garage sale more than the corporate marketplace it has become. He has watched every major transformation firsthand — the death of PayPal independence, the rise of managed payments, the overseas flooding that gutted the dropshipping model, the algorithm changes that rewarded professional sellers and squeezed out everyone else. This book is what twenty-plus years of adapting to those changes looks like when written down.

Before eBay selling became part of his work, Richard spent two decades as Director of Computer Operations at Trader Joe's, where he built the technology infrastructure supporting the company's growth from regional curiosity to national brand. That background — running systems at scale, watching what happens when platforms prioritize extraction over service — informed how he thinks about eBay's transformation and what sellers need to survive it.

Richard is also a professional ghostwriter with 113 published books to his credit, including works for Fortune 50 executives, technology founders, and industry leaders across finance, healthcare, and enterprise software. His clients have raised over $30 million in venture capital, earned TEDx invitations, and built platforms reaching millions of readers. His books have been adopted as university textbooks and translated into seven languages.

When not writing or selling, he collects vintage items — the kind that remind him why he started doing this in the first place. He lives in Florida and works with business leaders who have a story worth telling and want it told well. Learn more at TheWritingKing.com.

Books by Richard Lowe

See books by Richard Lowe at
https://masterofworlds.com

Get free publishing insights and industry updates at
https://thewritingking.substack.com

For ghostwriting and book coaching services see
https://thewritingking.com